HENRY VIII AND THE ENGLISH REFORMATION

DATE DUE

PROBLEMS IN EUROPEAN CIVILIZATION

HENRY VIII AND THE ENGLISH REFORMATION

EDITED WITH AN INTRODUCTION BY

Arthur J. Slavin

UNIVERSITY OF CALIFORNIA,
LOS ANGELES

D. C. HEATH AND COMPANY
A DIVISION OF
RAYTHEON EDUCATION COMPANY
LEXINGTON, MASSACHUSETTS

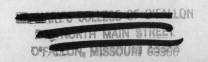

For my father and mother

Library of Congress Catalog Number: 68-29145

Printed in the United States of America

Table of Contents

Introduction

THERE ARE SEVERAL clearly defined traditions of historical writing about the English Reformation. The purpose of this volume is to describe and define these traditions, to trace their development over the centuries, and thereby to provide the reader with an introduction to the tantalizing problem of English Reformation history.

The traditions may be identified for these purposes as the Protestant, the Catholic, the *Politique,* and the school of the "New History." But a word of explanation is necessary here, if simplifications are to be understood properly. The words "Protestant" and "Catholic" clearly identify *partisan* religious stances in Reformation historiography. As we shall soon see with regard to Henry VIII himself, these terms may also often be said to imply others: hero and villain, for example. Also, by an extension of that implication historians of either persuasion have also seen More, Wolsey, Cranmer, and Cromwell in similar terms. Indeed, the quartet named have cast shadows upon historians' pages nearly as large as that of the king himself.

The term *"Politique"* as used here does not mean a tradition in which the historian is indifferent to religion or has no confessional loyalties. What it does refer to is that segment of the historical literature about the Henrician Reformation in which the historian's primary concern has *not* been the fate of the Church and its doctrine or ritual but the impact of the Reformation upon the English constitution and government. By the term "New History" is meant that growing school of Reformation historians whose frame of reference is not primarily religious, political, or biographical. Instead scholars of this school are chiefly concerned with the impact of Reformation upon English culture and society. That impact may be manifested in Renaissance literature, socioeconomic change, man's liberty in relation to authority, or the consequences of Reformation for particular institutions in Tudor England.

Such neat distinctions, however, are almost impossible to maintain. Since historians rarely, if ever, blind themselves to considerations other than character, if they are biographers; or religion, if they are church historians; or popular religion, if they are students of education and the transmission of ideas; or foreign affairs, if they are historians of the constitution — it will sometimes be difficult to put any one writer in one tradition and keep him there. Allowances must always be made in these matters, and rigid classification must not become a hindrance to the appreciation of the fine shadings of interpretation to be found in all schools.

The Catholic tradition itself has had a long history and is represented here by the work of Polydore Vergil, Sanders, Lingard, Constant, Hughes, and Knowles. But as quickly becomes evident, Vergil, Lingard, and Knowles are not *apologists* for a religious tradition in the same sense that Sanders, Constant, and Hughes are. Furthermore, Knowles may fairly be said to represent the "New History" in many ways, while Constant fits easily among the *Politiques.* While both are Catholic historians and in holy orders, the one is primarily interested in the institutional and cultural dimensions of monasticism in a Christian society, and the other in the ecclesiastical and civil polity of England.

Whatever we may think of the historians to whom we can justly give the title "Catholic," it very quickly becomes evident that there are wide divergences even within that tradition. One quickly senses the detachment of Polydore Vergil, the Renaissance man of letters who doubled as a papal tax gatherer in England. As a foreigner his moderation perhaps owed as much to his being Henry VIII's contemporary as it did to the fact that he lived his life more under Tudor patronage than in papal courts. The contrast between Vergil and Sanders is absolute; in Sanders' book one catches the intensity of feeling of the expatriate English Jesuit, more Roman than the pope, and one for whom the liturgical cadences of the seminary counted for more than did "Humanist Harry's" love of learning. In Sanders we first encounter that interpretation of Henry VIII as evil incarnate which recurs as a fainter but persistent echo in the more modern adherents to the Catholic view.

Lingard was a priest trained at Douay whose work, moderate in its censure of Henry VIII, was written in the very decades in which Catholic emancipation in England was to create the climate in which a more detached Catholic view of the 1530's become possible. That is not to say that even the most "scientific" Catholic historians often approach Henry VIII or the break with Rome without a certain melancholy sense of the loss of order. But it does seem that as the Catholic tradition has developed Catholics themselves have come to admit the necessity of reform, even while perhaps maintaining the traditional repugnance toward the king and his helpers in that enterprise and toward the vulgarity of the *error* which equated schism with reformation.

In that content Dom David Knowles' great work will repay time spent in deep reading many times over. His careful study of monks and monasteries exhibits modern Catholic scholarship at its very best. He escapes from simplistic explanations of the catastrophe which befell Rome in England and in so doing also escapes the easy equation in which Henry's will, perdition, and reform were once all equal terms. A close comparison of his work with that of his exact contemporary, Father Hughes, will

illustrate the richness of their tradition. The one sees in Wolsey the ruin of the Church in England. The other asks whether the Church had not failed in its purpose not because of a proud prelate but because for too long it had embraced the world too readily.

The theme giving unity to the historians who stand in the Protestant tradition as defined above may justly be described as the "providential" view of the Henrician Reformation. Hall, Lord Herbert of Cherbury, Bishop Burnet, the great Victorians Froude and Stubbs, and perhaps even Pollard shared the belief that when the Reformation came it was the king's work and that in doing it he was truly acting as a minister of God in putting Antichrist to rout.

Apart from this common view of God's providence, the Protestant historians have little enough in common. Hall is the sole contemporary witness of the events he describes and his chronicle, so closely followed by Shakespeare in the history plays, remains a vital source for Reformation historians. His own legal training and parliamentary experience were coupled with anticlerical sentiments and an adulation of the king which in themselves provided a framework for subsequent writers. All the Protestant historians accept an analysis which juxtaposes a Roman Church sufficiently decadent to necessitate reform and a king sufficiently learned and incisive to lead Parliament in that direction. They also see the king carefully playing upon popular resentments of clerical abuses, superstition, and fear of Roman jurisdiction irresponsibly exercised. From Hall to Pollard (who can on other grounds be considered in the *Politique* tradition) the Protestant historians have seen Henry VIII as the champion of of a just war justly fought.

That is not to say that all of the Protestant writers who depict Henry as the defender of truth, progress, and the national interest approved of all aspects of his character. To Hall he was a genuine hero and unsullied. Herbert of Cherbury, however, saw in Henry enough vice to make him wish that he could leave the king in his grave. An ardent royalist, writing at a time when the publication of a life of Henry (1647) might have been construed as a defense of the royal prerogative against the revolutionaries bent on subduing Charles I, Herbert did not allow the publication of his vindication of royalism during his lifetime. In many ways indifferent to partisan religious considerations, the "Father of English Deism" may well be the earliest of the *Politique* historians. Like Pollard, he shares a "providential" view of the Reformation. But it is a far cry from their tepid religious enthusiasms to the quiet but powerful intensity of a Burnet, Froude, or Stubbs.

The members of this last named trio are themselves quite dissimilar as historians of the Reformation. Bishop Burnet was no High Church partisan. A champion of toleration, an admirer of Thomas More, and a critic of Restoration, court society, and intrigues, his *History* mirrored his moderation. It is nevertheless unmistakably a Protestant view of things, in which the just triumph over the wicked despite the spotted character of their royal leader. Content to leave Henry's "scruple of conscience" to God, Burnet fastens on the king's minister, Thomas Cromwell, as the architect of concrete reforms and thereby begins a line of explanation which runs parallel to that deifying the king.

Froude was perhaps the most powerful spokesman for the royal genius. Emphasizing always Henry's Erasmian moderation in religious matters — a thing congenial to his nonconformist views of the High Church of his own day — the greatest literary historian of Reformation England all but apotheosized Henry VIII. His theme was that Henry was not only the maker of the modern English nation but that he was a worthy maker as well. What mattered a blemish here or a wart there in a figure and face of real majesty? in the life of the ruler who civilized Ireland, absorbed Wales and the Franchises into "the English system," raised the House of Commons to its greatness, subdued Rome, and managed an elegant and learned court in the bargain? Pollard, Henry's greatest biographer, would give all of that to the king. But he also wondered whether the architect of the modern constitution, the hero of Protestantism and progress, was not also the embodiment of the callousness of his age. But still he ends up evoking the spirit of the times to justify the king's actions and maintain against earlier historians that Henry's "tyranny" merely responded to a hunger men then felt for a state grown "to lusty manhood." Overcoming his Victorian sensibilities, Pollard, along with Stubbs (who was an impeccably rigorous member of the Anglican episcopate) glorified the king in contrast to Thomas More and Fisher — who represented "only individual conscience" against the state, the "New Messiah." Stubbs did see Henry's "grotesque and inhuman self absorption"; but his great qualities gave to his exercise of power in the crisis of the 1530's the color of justice. He *evolved* the notion of a "regal papacy," itself a divinely appointed task, while to Cromwell went the credit for most of the evil which existed in England between 1529 and 1540.

Pollard's insistence on the epoch-making aspects of Henry's revolution in church and state clearly qualify him among the historians whose main interests lie in government and constitutional change. He, Herbert, and Elton may be described as *Politiques*. Herbert was primarily interested in the relationship between character and events. Pollard and Elton, on the other hand, are primarily concerned with the significance of events in the interpretation of what Elton has called the "Tudor Revolution." For them the king's character may also be an abiding concern — each has written about it at some length — but both of them agree that the really crucial point is that the Reformation brought to an end the medieval phase of England's history.

Insistent in that agreement, they find themselves in accord in little else. While Pollard stands in the train of Froude, emphasizing that the king came of age upon Wolsey's fall in 1529 and himself planned and executed the revolution of the 1530's,

Elton argues that Thomas Cromwell was the true political genius of the age in England. The minister, not the king, designed and pushed through the program of reforms that together constituted a radical break with the past — a revolution. Despite this basic disagreement, it seems true to say that they are in agreement that the most important aspect of the Reformation is its role in the birth of the modern state. On this point both the Protestant and *Politique* traditions are linked to Catholics of the opinion of Hughes and Constant. In that affinity the question of hero-villain is perhaps a clue to the general interpretation of events as dependent upon the works of a genius — king or minister, malign or glorious.

This concern with personalities in relationship to the government and constitution of the church and the state does not figure largely in the work of the "New History," except perhaps in a negative way. This can perhaps best be seen in Douglas Bush's essay on "Tudor Humanism and Henry VIII." While concerned with the king's role in the executions of Thomas More and Bishop Fisher, Bush writes about the impact of the Reformation on the life of learning and literature. And his constant concern is to show that stimulation rather than sedation was the outcome of the crisis brought on by the king's great matter. From this concern with education and literature to Dickens' inquiries into the origins of English Protestantism is but a short jump in the "New History." The examinations of Bush and Dickens have this in common: both are concerned with real, concrete people as the objects to whom reform is either relevant or a waste of time and motion. While Dickens certainly has sympathy with the Reformers and may with some justice be called a "Protestant" historian, the center of gravity of his work is low. His eye is on the people of the parishes in the diocese of York, not on high, at the court or in the relationships between kings and ministers. It is typical of the broad social concern of the recent historians of Reformation England that they always inquire about the "country" as well as the court.

In that regard Christopher Hill is especially interesting. Bringing to bear upon the legislation of the 1530's a telescope rather than a microscope, he looks into the distant future and sees there the dramatic consequences of certain Tudor social and economic star-bursts. Agreeing with the *Politiques* that the "revolution" of the 1530's was an act of state, Hill maintains that the wide spread of Protestantism was a consequence, not a cause, of the Reformation. Granting to religious partisans that this was the most immediate important result of the Reformation, he argues strenuously that social and economic shifts were inherent in Henry VIII's confiscation and redistribution of Church wealth as well as in his challenge to traditional religions' authoritarianism. The implications of these events slowly manifested themselves in the century after Thomas Cromwell's death (1540). It is Hill's view that another revolutionary of the same family name, the future Protector Oliver Cromwell, was a product of the dialectic necessity which required that political power be brought into harmony with the earlier redistribution of wealth. Thus ironically the door left ajar by the Henrician attacks on Rome was opened wide in popular attacks on the monarchy and Parliament.

Thus we end where we began — with the analysis of a historian whose apparent indifference to religion leads to the primacy of politics and the constitution. But what different roads Polydore Vergil and Christopher Hill have traversed! Having worked through the "cult of personality" through the "character" writers, through centuries of partisan religious historiography and the *Politiques,* we end with a self-confessed Marxist analysis in which both religion and economics serve as handmaidens to a historical muse dressed in the cloak of constitutionalism.

* * *

All footnotes to these articles are those of the editor of this volume, not of the authors of the articles.

AN EXTRAORDINARY PRETEXT

POLYDORE VERGIL

This humanist and papal collector in England was born about 1470 in
Urbino and was educated at Bologna and Padua. His career was based on
secretarial service to the Duke of Urbino and a chamberlain's part at the court
of the infamous Borgia pope Alexander VI. Between 1502 and 1551 he lived
chiefly in England, where he enjoyed numerous church preferments as well as
Wolsey's hostility. He became "naturalized" in 1510. His important works
were an edition of the fabulous history of Gildas, a collection of proverbs
anticipating the *Adagia* of Erasmus, and a work of lasting interest to historians
of science and technology, *De Inventoribus Rerum*. *Anglica Historia* was begun
at Henry VII's urging in 1505. The 1555 edition carried the work on from
1509 to 1538 and provides a contemporary view of the crisis of the 1530's.

Now WAS imminent that calamity which was to fall upon Wolsey, when, like an untamed horse, he was unable to stay quiet. For it came into his head to change his queen and to find a new one, whom he wished to be like him in conduct and character; and this although Queen Catherine did not hurt or damage the fellow, but, hating his evil ways, had sometimes gently admonished him to cultivate self-control. Certain of achieving this plan as soon as it had occurred to him, he had a friendly discussion concerning a future enquiry with John Longland bishop of Lincoln, because the latter was the person who heard the king's confession. The bishop, who said that in his own opinion he did nothing dishonourable but only acted correctly, had already for a long time considered that the royal marriage should be dissolved as invalid and had often whispered this view in secret to his intimates; he listened to Wolsey with such exceeding willingness that both soon began to discuss together whether the marriage of Henry and Catherine was legally binding or not. Taking upon themselves more than was proper, as if they had been most learned theologians but with more presumption,

they looked for difficulties where there were none (as the saying is), and readily decided that the marriage was neither valid nor sound, on the grounds that Catherine had previously married Henry's brother Arthur. Agreeing with one another in this opinion, they decided it should promptly be revealed to the king that such a matrimonial state was most perilous, just as though the doubt which from the start had been provoked by that earlier relationship had not yet been removed from men's minds. This plan having been adopted, Wolsey decided to take the duty upon himself. At a convenient moment he approached the king and with an appearance of affection and love of righteousness warned him of the legal standing of such a marriage. He went on to assert that it had no force or vigour because of the marriage Catherine had made with his brother and he urgently besought him no longer to live in such peril since upon it directly depended the salvation of his soul, the legitimacy of the royal issue, the decency of his life. When he heard this, the king for a little was speechless, greatly astonished that his marriage should be condemned, because originally it had been approved as just and

From Polydore Vergil, *Anglica Historia* (London, 1950), pp. 325–37. Reprinted by permission of The
Royal Historical Society, the Camden Society, and Denys Hay, editor and translator.

1

worthy by the pope and the most important and learned bishops and had been
solemnised at their wishes. Then the king
said: "Good father, mark well how (as the
proverb puts it) you are trying to move a
stone which is already lying in its place.
For I have as a wife a most noble woman
and one who is most excellent and devout,
against whom nothing can be objected
which could merit a divorce. That you say
she was married to my brother presents no
difficulty, since she has herself often in the
past testified on oath that she never had
carnal knowledge of him on account of his
youth and impotence." So on that occasion
only a brief discussion ensued on the matter. But three days afterwards, Wolsey,
shielded by his most brazen effrontery, summoned the bishop of Lincoln and took him
to the king, whom the bishop thus ad-
dressed: "We stand before you, most excellent prince, to do our duty, and especially
that I should. Since by now it cannot have
escaped you that the people have grown to
regard your marriage as doubtful and uncertain, we have investigated the matter.
Since it is evident enough that there are
defects in it, therefore I, whose charge it is
to think of your soul, beseech, implore and
urge you to decide at last upon committing
the affair to a judicial enquiry by which
it may become apparent to all how the case
stands, and so that you may thus be said to
cherish righteousness as is always your custom." This argument seemed just, decent
and sound to Henry, and it began to dispose him towards the investigation of this
question. Thereupon Wolsey, who considered the whole matter to be as good as settled, to encourage the king to arrange a
divorce at the earliest moment, said: "There
is a woman who is more worthy than the
rest to marry you, the widowed sister of
King Francis of France; she was the wife of
the duke of Alençon and is a most splendid
creature both in her youth and her virtue."[1]
"Such matters," said Henry then, "are for

greater consideration and therefore I am
sure should be deferred to another time."
Now when news of the future enquiry
came to Catherine's ears she was utterly
plunged into grief and mourning; she lamented, and bewailed that she should have
survived so long only for such a desperately
afflicting misfortune. But the king com-
forted her, asserting that the trial of the
matter would assuredly establish the truth.

During this time news arrived that Pope
Clement had fallen under the control of
the imperial troops. This intelligence indeed gave more of a shock to Wolsey than
anyone else, because he now feared for his
legateship. He began to urge King Henry
to decide upon aiding with all his resources
and support the common father of all Christians, and when he realised the king cared
very little about it, he thus argued the matter: "Most gracious prince, since you are
'Defender of the Faith' it is in the highest
degree your concern to protect the governor, guardian and head of the faith, this is,
of our religion."[2] To this Henry replied:
"If the Roman pope had fought in the
cause of religion and not temporal power, I
should have considered that to be my
course of action. But so that it may be
clear and apparent to all that the safety of
the pope is my responsibility, you shall
without delay go to Francis king of France
and on my behalf urge him to resolve upon
sending the army which he has prepared
to Italy, in order to force the imperialists
to set the pope free; and in my name you
shall arrange to pay a proportion of the expenses." This having been arranged, and
the two of them keeping it as a secret,
Wolsey arranged to make the journey he
desired with speed. Then it spread about
and began to be on everyone's lips and in
everyone's talk, that he was going to France
to take money for a campaign against the
emperor and to bring back with him the
French king's sister to marry Henry. They
said that these sayings were spread abroad

---

[1] Vergil is in error. It was not Francis I's sister
Margaret but his sister-in-law Princess Renée who
was proposed for Henry VIII.

[2] In October 1521 this title was conferred on
Henry VIII by Pope Leo X, as a reward for his
Defense of the Seven Sacraments.

by Wolsey's crafty care, so that it might be rumoured that the marriage between the king and Catherine was now openly discredited. Thereafter Wolsey took two associates in his mission to discuss matters with Francis — the bishop of London, recently returned from Spain, and William Sandys the lord chamberlain. In great style he went to Amiens. There, gracious heavens! so friendly was his reception by King Francis, so courteous and worthy his treatment, he might have been no other than a king! At the same place he was also entertained with great courtesy by Louise, the king's mother. Afterwards business began; first a war plan was discussed to compel the imperialists by force to give Pope Clement his liberty and no small sum was allocated for this purpose; then for some days there were negotiations concerning the establishment of a treaty and other very secret matters, in which conference, indeed, Wolsey's two colleagues participated so little that they openly admitted after they returned that they did not know what matters Wolsey had transacted with the French king. From this the suspicion sprang that a fresh marriage for Francis's sister had been discussed and that that matter had been arranged and agreed, as Wolsey himself boasted. Yet the princess was in fact a worthy woman, and would hear nothing of the marriage, since such a marriage could not take place without wretched ruin and even destruction for Catherine. Now Wolsey with matters arranged happily (so he said), returned to England and at his pleasure carefully reported his mission to the king, who was glad to learn of both what had been done and what remained to be done, for the advantage of himself and his allies. In addition, so as the alliance of the kings should be strengthened by an even closer association, Francis at this time was made a member of the Order of the Garter, and Henry of the Order of St. Michael, which is the most sacred and honourable distinction among the French. This year was the nineteenth of Henry's reign, and 1527 of human salvation, and in it Pope

Clement obtained his freedom without any aid or assistance from King Francis, who greedily put in his own coffers the money which he had shortly before received from Wolsey for the projected help. Henry was extremely pleased that Pope Clement had been given his liberty by his enemies and wrote to congratulate him. While Henry thus observed the tumult of war gradually dying down abroad, at home he was at last attending to the conduct of his own most serious and unpleasant affairs, as we shall show below. It was then that he chose Stephen Gardiner,[3] a doctor of law, and a man of the highest intelligence, as his confidential secretary and thereafter relied greatly on his services. Richard Pace[4] had held this office with the king, but he was worn down by being frequently sent on embassies (many of which were not at all necessary but given him by Wolsey so that he should be away all the longer from the king); suffering from virtual exile from his native land, his mind as a result was so impaired that he shortly after began to have periods of madness.

At the start of the very next year, the king and queen, although against both their wills, embarked on legal proceedings. The case going to court and the action beginning, both parties were given the most skilled lawyers and theologians, as well as proctors and experienced advocates. The king in the meantime, who acted entirely in good faith so that the truth of the matter should be revealed and the legitimate royal issue thus be established, wrote to the pope asking him to send a legate to England to hear the case. He also sent his proctors to all the universities of France and Italy in order to urge the scholars most learned in law to give their opinion on his marriage,

---

[3] Wolsey's agent, Secretary of State, later Bishop of Winchester; a brilliant Cambridge lecturer, diplomat and politician who served Henry VIII and, after a long residence in the Tower under Edward VI, was Mary I's Lord Chancellor.

[4] This highly educated humanist Secretary of State was Wolsey's agent and the author of a treatise on education (*De Fructu*) critical of the nobility.

and to elucidate the matter through the written views of individuals. Soon after arrived the papal legate Cardinal Lorenzo Campeggio, who had Wolsey as his colleague. On an appointed day the two cardinals took their seats in the Dominican friary in London. King Henry first appeared before them and spoke concerning the business: "Most worthy fathers, I shall be brief. I have in marriage a wife Catherine who is most dear to me, both on account of the extraordinary virtues of her character and of her noble birth. But since I am ruler of a great kingdom, I have to be sure whether I may rightly, legally, honourably and piously live with her, and have children by her, to whom the inheritance of this realm may descend on the soundest legal grounds. Both questions will be resolved if you determine that our marriage is valid. But if there is any doubt in the matter, I beg that you will reveal it by your authority or annul it; so that in this matter both my conscience and the minds of my subjects may for ever be set at rest." Then the queen appeared and publicly accused Wolsey most solemnly of treachery, deceit, injustice and evil-doing in creating dissension between herself and her husband. She accordingly said openly: "I deny, revolt from and shun such a judge, who is the bitterest enemy both of me and of law and justice; and I appeal solely to the pope, placing the judgment of my case in his hands." As she tearfully said these words, you could see Wolsey being regarded by nearly everyone with hostile looks. And so the hearing of the case was suspended. Nevertheless the legates often sat thereafter in their judicial capacity, both dealing with those matters which related to the furnishing of proofs in the case, and seeking if by some agreement the queen would revoke her appeal — which she persistently refused to do. But because the legates wasted time since they came to no decision, the suspicion then occurred to the king that they behaved thus on purpose, to bring the business to naught in their court. While things were going on in this way, Wolsey, who was a shrewd man, realised that Henry had cast his eyes on a girl called Anne, the daughter of Thomas Boleyn viscount Rochford, and one of the queen's maids-in-waiting. Then Wolsey was very greatly perturbed, foreseeing that it would come about that the king would marry her if the divorce were obtained. Accordingly he at once began with great energy and all care and diligence to arrange, provide and ensure that such an event by no means came about; for he considered it would be more to be avoided than death, because of the arrogance of the girl. With matters thus arranged and the case of Catherine to be heard and judged in Rome (maintaining the appeal which she had made there), Wolsey secretly urged Pope Clement by letters and by private envoys to withhold judgment on the divorce, until he should have firmly turned Henry's mind to his own way of thinking. Yet nothing was brought about by these devices which could remain hidden from the king, who therefore decided to reduce to the lowest ranks this man who was so forgetful of his favours. So first he sent Cardinal Campeggio away in friendly fashion, and then soon after ordered Thomas duke of Norfolk to go to Wolsey, to strip him of all his dignities and wealth and to take him to a manor of the bishop of Winchester, called Esher.[5] In this place he remained for some months, and finally was banished to his diocese of York that he might there learn to lead a better and a more modest life. Far from this ensuing, it happened that he was in no way able to subdue the passions of his corrupt nature because the punishment of his sins now encompassed him. The idea came to him to go to York, there to take his place on the pontifical throne in triumphal fashion, as is the custom, and for many days after to be filled with the pomp of ceremonies, banquets and games — he whom compassion was already beginning to befriend sought thus to be an object of envy. And because he lacked valuable vestments, clothed in which he would seem

[5] Wolsey had been deprived of his bishopric of Winchester upon his fall in the autumn of 1529.

grander, he therefore did not hesitate to write asking Henry to provide him with the mitre and pall which he had formerly been accustomed to use in celebrating the divine office. When he read this letter, the king could not but greatly marvel at Wolsey's brazen insolence, saying: "Is there still arrogance in this fellow, who is so obviously ruined?" But since preparations were on foot everywhere in the province, both of the matters and the men involved in the solemnities, the king decided to be tolerant no further. He ordered Henry, earl of Northumberland, to take Wolsey into custody in order to stop him becoming haughtier and acting like a madman. While Wolsey was soon afterwards being taken to London, he was completely overcome and died at the town of Leicester; in that place he was buried. How uncertain is the lot of man at birth! How equally inconstant in living! Wolsey flourished in importance and wealth: when he set in motion the marriage project, which he considered would be a fine thing for him, it brought him ruin. This was the year 1530 of human salvation, the twenty-second of Henry's reign. Stephen Gardiner was then made bishop of Winchester, who subsequently devoted himself more to the study of sacred literature, in which he soon made such progress that he became a splendid preacher. Immediately afterwards he undertook a protracted mission at the court of Francis king of France.

After these events, the divorce between Henry and Catherine ensued in the following way. While the case of Catherine's appeal (which we have recorded above) was being dealt with at the papal court, the archbishop of Canterbury,[6] together with his bishops in a body and a crowd of attorneys, put his sickle to another man's harvest, as the common saying is. He came to the village of Dunstable, within a distance of six miles from the royal manor called Ampthill, where Catherine was staying at the time. Here she was cited on

successive days. When after the fifteenth day, she had neither appeared nor made answer to the judge (since he was irregular), the divorce was suddenly accomplished!. Henry left Catherine and married Anne Boleyn, whom he had a little earlier begun to love, and by whom he had a daughter, Elizabeth by name. Meanwhile a parliament was held in London, in which the English church assumed a political organisation never seen in former ages; for Henry was established as head of the church itself, and in respect of this office the first fruits of all vacant livings and the annual tenth of these livings were allocated to him for ever.

A method of dealing with legal actions was also established; the defendant had first to appeal to his bishop, then to the archbishop and finally to the king himself; so thus there was absolutely no need of the authority of the pope in the administration of any matters concerning the church. However, this enactment was at first certainly not approved of by everyone, especially not by John Fisher, bishop of Rochester, a man of great learning and the highest honour and piety, nor by Sir Thomas More, so greatly distinguished in his writings and in his virtuous life. Together they finally preferred to abandon their lives rather than their convictions, in the belief that they would all the sooner delight eternally in heaven; and a few others chose to act likewise. In the same parliament provision was furthermore made with the greatest care and application, that this very power, which had been already seized on an extraordinary pretext, should in the future be maintained and protected. Through this power Henry decreed the adoption in England of new religious observances and very different ways of worshipping God, and at the same time the reduction of monastic establishments and the diminution of the property of other priests, lest more extravagance should thereafter result. Wherefore after it seemed that sufficient provision had been made for the ratification and confirmation of all these actions, laws were enacted and

6 Thomas Cranmer.

the severest penalties laid down for those who acted against what was required by these laws, or who by any unlawful word or saying impugned the acts and ordinances of the parliament. But we must return to Catherine. After the divorce from her husband had been accomplished, she went to a royal house in Bedfordshire, which is called Kimbolton, a most unhealthy spot; there, wonderfully fortified by a deep resignation, she led a life of piety. When later, however, her spirit worn out with grief, she began to ail, Henry heard of this and promptly persuaded Eustache Chapuys, the imperial ambassador, to see her and give her the good wishes of the king. Eustache performed this duty with both diligence and speed. Yet six days later Catherine became more seriously ill. When she realised that death approached she ordered an educated maid-in-waiting to write two letters in the same tenor, one to the king and the other to Eustache. She dictated these in the following words:

My lord king and ever dearest husband, greetings: The hour of my death now approaches, and at this moment my love compels me to remind you a little of the salvation of your soul. This last you should put before all mortal considerations, abandoning on this account all those concerns of the flesh on account of which you have plunged both me into manifold miseries and yourself into more anxieties. Yet this I forgive you, and I both hope and with holy prayers implore that God will forgive you. For the rest, I commend the daughter of our marriage to your care, whom I beseech you to behave towards entirely in that fatherly fashion which I have on other occasions desired of you. I specially pray you also to take care of my maids and to see that at the right time they are given good husbands (which is not much to ask, for there are only three of them); and out of your grace, good will and generosity to pay my servants the salaries due them and also for a further year, lest they should seem to be forsaken or in want. Lastly I have only one thing to declare: that my eyes long for you above all else. Farewell.

And in the letter to Eustache she added that, if Henry did not fulfil her dying requests, he should arrange for the emperor to remind the king of his duty. On the same day she died, 6 January in the year of salvation 1535 and the twenty-seventh of Henry's reign. When the king read this letter, he burst into affectionate tears. For who could be so hard and unbending, but would not be stirred by being the object of such pure and earnest benevolence. The body of this most worthy queen was carried to Peterborough and honourably buried in the Benedictine monastery. Now we may further trace marriage matters. Queen Anne rejoiced at the death of Catherine the consort of her royal husband, because there could be no further dispute concerning that marriage. The king likewise was in high hopes of becoming the father thereafter of more children, and especially boys, for which he was anxious above all, since his wife was pregnant. But mark how quickly the course of good fortune is interrupted! For Anne soon after being taken in adultery suffered capital punishment together with her paramours.

Then Henry took as his wife, Jane, the very excellent daughter of Sir John Seymour, a woman of the utmost charm both in appearance and character. By her Henry became father of Edward VI, who now reigns. He is a youth who most assuredly was destined for rule, for virtue and for wisdom. He is endowed with the highest talents and has aroused the greatest expectations among all men. His mother, however, died in childbirth, two days after she had been delivered. She gave birth on 13 October in the thirtieth year of Henry's reign, and of human salvation 1538.[7]

---

[7] Again, Vergil is in error. Jane Seymour gave birth to the future Edward VI on October 12, 1537.

THE ROYAL REFORMER: AN APOLOGY

EDWARD HALL

The contemporary historian of Henry VIII's reign, Edward Hall, was born late in the fifteenth or early in the sixteenth century. From Eton he went to King's College, Cambridge, where he took a B.A. in 1518. He read law at Gray's Inn and served as a common serjeant-at-law and a member of parliament. He also was a commissioner to inquire into abuses of the Six Articles between 1541 and 1544. His work *The Union of the Noble and Illustre famelies of Lancaster and York* dates to 1542 and is often informed about affairs in which Hall played an active part. Followed closely by Shakespeare, prohibited by Queen Mary, it came to be recognized as a valuable, if partisan, source, especially after being reprinted early in the nineteenth century. Hall died in 1547.

THE xxiiii. day of December, the kinges majestie came into the parliament house, to geve his royal assent, to suche actes as there had passed, where was made unto him by the Speaker, an eloquent oration, to the which it hath ever ben accustomed, that the lord Chauncellor[1] made answere, but at this time it was the kynges pleasure, that it should be otherwyse, for the kyng himself made him answer, as foloweth worde for worde, as nere as I was able to report it.

"Although my Chauncelor for the time beyng, hath before this time used, very eloquently and substancially, to make answer to suche oracions, as hath bene set furth in this high court of Parliamente, yet is he not so able to open and set furth my mynd and meanyng, and the secretes of my hart, in so plain and ample maner, as I my selfe am and can do: wherfore I taking upon me, to answer your eloquent oracion maister Speaker, say, that wher you, in the name of our welbeloved commons hath both praysed and extolled me, for the notable qualities, that you have conceived to be in me, I most hartely thanke you all, that you have put me in remembraunce of my dutye, whiche is to endevor my self to obtein and get suche excellent qualities, and necessary vertues, as a Prince or governor, should or ought to have, of which giftes I recognise my self, bothe bare and barrein: but of suche small qualities, as God hathe endued me withal, I rendre to his goodnes my moste humble thankes, entendyng with all my witte and diligence, to get and acquire to me suche notable vertues, and princely qualities, as you have alleged to be incorporate in my persone: These thankes for your lovyng admonicion and good counsaill firste remembred, I eftsones thanke you again, because that you consideryng our greate charges (not for our pleasure, but for your defence, not for our gain, but to our great cost) whiche we have lately susteined, aswell in defence of our and your enemies, as for the conquest of that fortresse, which was to this realme, moste displeasaunt and noysome, and shalbe by Goddes grace hereafter, to our nacion moste profitable and pleasaunt, have frely of youre awne mynde, graunted to us a certain subsedy, here in an act specified, whiche verely we take in good part, re-

[1] Thomas Lord Wriothesley, who succeeded Sir Thomas Audley May 3, 1544, and, as the Earl of Southampton, was relieved March 7, 1547.

From Edward Hall, *Henry VIII* (London, 1904), pp. 354–58.

garding more your kindnes, then the proffite thereof, as he that setteth more by your loving hartes, then by your substaunce. Beside this hartie kindnes, I cannot a litle rejoyse when I consider, the perfite trust and sure confidence, whiche you have put in me, as men having undoubted hope, and unfeined belefe in my good dooynges, and just procedinges for you, without my desire or request, have committed to myne ordre and disposicion, all Chauntryes, Colleges, Hospitalles, and other places specefied in a certain act,[2] firmely trustyng that I wil ordre them to the glory of God, and the profite of the common wealth. Surely if I contrary to your expectacion, shuld suffre the ministres of the Church to decaie, or learnyng (whiche is so great a juell) to be minished, or pore and miserable people, to be unrelieved, you might say that I beyng put in so speciall a trust, as I am in this cace, were no trustie frende to you, nor charitable man to mine even christian, neither a lover of the publyk wealth, nor yet one that feared God, to whom accompt must be rendered of all our doynges. Doubt not I praye you, but your expectacion shalbe served, more Godly and goodly then you wil wish or desire, as hereafter you shall plainly perceive.

"Now, sithence I find suche kyndenes, on your part towarde me, I can not chose, but love and favor you, affirmyng that no prince in the world, more favoreth his subjectes, then I do you, nor no subjectes or commons more, love and obaye, their sovereigne lord, then I perceive you do me, for whose defence my treasure shal not be hidden, nor yf necessitye requyre my persone shall not bee unadventured: yet although I with you, and you with me, be in this perfect love and concord, this frendly amity can not continue, except bothe you my lordes temporal, and you my lordes spiritual, and you my lovyng subjectes, studie and take paine to amend one thing, which surely is amisse, and farre out of ordre, to the which I moste hartely require you,

whiche is, that charity and concord is not amongst you, but discord and dissencion, beareth rule in every place. S. Paule saieth to the Corinthians, in the xiii. Chapiter, Charitie is gentle, Charitie is not envious, Charitie is not proude and so furth in the said Chapiter: Beholde then what love and Charitie is emongest you, when the one calleth the other, Hereticke and Anabaptist, and he calleth hym again Papist, Ypocrite, and Pharisey. Be these tokens of charitie emongest you? Are these the signes of fraternal love betwen you? No, no, I assure you, that this lacke of Charitie emongest your selfes, will bee the hinderaunce and asswagyng, of the fervent love betwene us, as I said before, except this wound be salved, and clerely made whole. I must nedes judge the faut and occasion of this discorde, to bee partly by negligence of you the fathers and preachers of the spiritualtie. For if I know a man whyche liveth in adultery, I muste judge hym a lecherous and a carnall persone: If I se a man boast and bragg hymself, I cannot but deme hym a proude manne. I se and here daily that you of the Clergy preache one against another, teache one contrary to another, inveigh one against another without Charity or discrecion. Some be to styff in their old Mumpsimus, other be to busy and curious, in their newe Sumpsimus. Thus all men almoste be in variety and discord, and fewe or none preache truly and sincerely the worde of God, accordyng as thei ought to do. Shal I now judge you charitable persones doing this? No, no, I cannot so do: alas how can the pore soules live in concord when you preachers sow emonges them in your sermons, debate and discord? Of you thei loke for light, and you bryng them to darckenes. Amende these crymes I exhorte you, and set forth Goddes worde, bothe by true preaching, and good example gevyng, or els I whom God hath appoynted his Vicare, and high mynyster here, wyll se these dyvisions extinct, and these enormities corrected, according to my very duety, or els I am an unproffitable servaunte, and untrue officer.

[2] Dissolved by statute in 1545; but few were put down until the new "Chantries Act" of 1547.

"Although as I saie, the spirituall men be in some faute, that charytie is not kept emongest you, yet you of the temporaltie, bee not cleane and unspotted of malice and envie, for you rayle on Bishoppes, speake slaunderously of Priestes, and rebuke and taunt Preachers, bothe contrary to good ordre, and Christian fraternity. If you knowe surely that a bishop or preacher, erreth or techeth perverse doctrine, come and declare it to some of our Counsayl or to us, to whom is committed by God the high aucthority to reforme and ordre such causes and behaviours: and bee not Judges your selfes, of your awne phantasticall opinions, and vain exposicions, for in suche high causes ye maie lightly erre. And al though you be permitted to reade holy scripture, and to have the word of God in your mother tongue, you must understande that it is licensed you so to do, onely to informe your awne conscience, and to instruct your children and famely, and not to dispute and make scripture, a railyng and a tauntyng stocke, against Priestes and Preachers (as many light persones do).[3] I am very sory to knowe and here, how unreverently that moste precious juel the worde of God is disputed, rymed, song and jangeled in every Alehouse and Taverne, contrary to the true meaninge and doctrine of the same. And yet I am even asmuch sory, that the readers of the same, folowe it in doynge so fayntlye and coldly: for of thys I am sure, that Charitie was never so faint emongest you, and verteous and Godly livyng was never lesse used, nor God him self emongest Christians, was never lesse reverenced, honored or served. Therfore as I said before, bee in Charitie one with another, like brother and brother, love dread and serve God (to the which I as your supreme heade, and sovereigne lord, exhort and require you) and then I doubt not, but that love and league, that I spake of in the beginning, shall never be dissolved or broken betwene us. And the makynge of lawes, whiche be now made and concluded, I exhort you the makers, to bee as dilligent in puttyng them in execucion, as you wer in making and furthering the same, or els your labor shalbe in vain, and your common wealth nothing releved. Now to your peticion, concerning our royal assent, to be geven to such actes as hath passed both the houses. They shalbe read openly, that ye maye hear them." Then they were openly read, and to many hys grace assented, and diverse he assented not unto. Thys the kynges oracion was to his subjectes there present suche comfort, that the lyke joye could not be unto them in this world. And thus the actes read, as the maner is, and his assent geven, his grace rose and departed.

[3] The injunctions issued by Thomas Cromwell in 1536 and 1538 are here referred to by the king.

BY A JUST JUDGMENT OF GOD

NICHOLAS SANDERS

This vigorous polemicist and historian was born about 1530 and educated at New College, Oxford, where he was a fellow in 1548. Deserting England for Rome in Edward VI's reign, Nicholas Sanders became a priest in the course of legal and theological studies. He put his learning to work in a .Louvain professorship as well as in controversialist causes, especially against the moderate Anglican John Jewel's *De Visibili Monarchia Ecclesiae*. From 1573 to 1579 he was a papal *provocateur* against England, first in Madrid and then in Ireland, working always for Elizabeth's downfall. His historical manuscripts were printed only after his death in 1581.

WHEN THE KING saw, as the hour of death was approaching, that in his greed, or rather in his rage, he had broken away from the unity of the Church, he consulted secretly with some of the bishops how he might be reconciled to the Apostolic See, and the rest of Christendom. But behold the severity of God with those who knowingly fall into sin, or who lull themselve asleep therein! No man was found courageous enough to advise him honestly, to tell him his mind, or to show him the truth; they were all afraid because of his former cruelty. They knew that many had been put to death who had spoken their minds frankly in past times, either to him or to Cromwell, even those who had been commanded to speak. So was it now; one of the bishops, doubting whether a snare had been laid for him, replied, the king was far wiser than other men; he had, under the divine guidance, renounced the supremacy of the Roman Pontiff, and had nothing to be afraid of, now that his resolution had been confirmed by the public law of the realm.[1]

It is said, too, that Stephen Gardiner, bishop of Winchester, persuaded him, when alone with him, to call his Parliament together, if possible, and to communicate to it a matter of that importance; if the time was too short, then to express his resolution in writing, and thereby testify to the voice of his conscience, for God would be satisfied with the mere desire of his heart, if he were in any straits which necessarily hindered the performance of the act. But as soon as the bishop had gone, the crowd of flatterers came around him, and afraid that the return of the kingdom to the obedience of the Holy See would force them to part with the ecclesiastical lands, these men persuaded him to allow no such scruples to enter his mind. It is very easy for a man not rooted and grounded in charity to break a good resolution. The king's consultation with his bishops concerning the restoration of the kingdom to the unity of the Church had no other fruit than to show openly that he who, against his conscience, had broken away from the Roman Church, and was therefore resisting the known truth, had sinned against the Holy Ghost.

As to the temper, pursuits, and habits of the king, we may say briefly that he was not unversed in learning, that he encouraged learned men, and increased the sala-

[1] There is no contemporary authority for Henry VIII's supposed remorse.

From Nicholas Sanders, *The Rise and Growth of the Anglican Schism* (London, Burns and Oates: 1877), pp. 160–65.

ries of certain professors. With the exception of Cranmer, whom he made archbishop of Canterbury, to be the minister of his lust in the affair of the divorce, the bishops he named were men of learning, and very far from being bad men; many of them afterwards, during the reigns of Edward and Elizabeth, suffered bonds and imprisonment as confessors of the Catholic faith.

His reverence for the Sacrament of the Eucharist was always most profound. Shortly before he died, when about to communicate, as he always did, under one kind, he rose up from his chair, and fell on his knees to adore the Body of our Lord. The Zuinglians who were present said that his majesty, by reason of his bodily weakness, might make his communion sitting in his chair. The king's answer was, "If I could throw myself down, not only on the ground, but under the ground, I should not then think that I gave honour enough to the most Holy Sacrament."

He gave up the Catholic faith for no other reason in the world than that which came from his lust and wickedness. He rejected the authority of the Pope because he was not allowed to put away Catherine, when he was beaten and overcome as he was by the flesh. He destroyed the monasteries, partly because the monks, and especially the friars, resisted the divorce; partly because he hungered after the ecclesiastical lands, which he seized that he might have more abundant means to spend in feasting on women of unclean lives, and on the foolish buildings he raised.

His understanding was acute, and his judgment solid, whenever he applied himself to the serious discussion of any question, especially in the early part of the day. After dinner he was often overcome with wine, and the courtiers, the flatterers, and the heretics with whom Anne Boleyn and others, both wives and concubines, had filled the court, observed it, and then never spoke to him for the purpose of their own advantage, or for that of ruining others, but in the afternoon. Others, too, waited for

the time when he took physic, for he was then more than usually cheerful; and there were those who allowed him to beat them or cheat them at dice — he was on such occasions demonstrative in his joy — and then hinting that they were ruined, begged of him in return either the goods of some innocent man, or the lead of a monastery,[2] or the bells of a church, or something of great price of that kind. It is said of one that he was not only rewarded, but raised to honours, because he gave the king a porkling well dressed, of which he was very fond; of another, because he moved the king's chair at the fitting moment away from the fire; and of another, because he behaved himself respectfully and pleasantly at dice.

He restored Mary, Catherine's child, to her rank, that she might be the next in succession to his son Edward, and take precedence of Elizabeth. It is very clear from this that he was dishonest in putting away his wife, and that he did so under the influence of his passion for Anne Boleyn. He appointed, by his last will, sixteen persons to be the guardians of his son, thereby making the monarchy, as it were, an aristocracy. Shortly before he died he ordered Thomas duke of Norfolk — he was one of those who had treated the Apostolic Legates with scant respect, though otherwise a Catholic[3] — to be imprisoned for life, and had the son of the duke, the earl of Surrey, beheaded. This he did, deceived by the heretics, who took care that those Catholics should be put out of the way, for it was not believed that they had committed any offence against the king.

The king having ruined a most admirable constitution by unsatiable gluttony, was now grown so unwieldy that he could hardly enter by the doors, and was wholly unable to mount up the stairs. They lifted him up, sitting in a chair, by machinery,

2 Henry VIII's fiscal expedients under the pressures of war and inflation did include selling off the lead stripped from church roofs and monastic buildings in general.

3 Norfolk was certainly violently antiecclesiastic, especially with regard to Wolsey.

to the upper rooms of the palace. It was said that he had no blood left in his body, that it was corrupted into humours. When he was told that he was at the point of death, he called for a goblet of white wine, and turning to one of his attendants said, "All is lost!"

He reigned thirty-seven years, nine months, and six days, nearly twenty years of which he passed in the peace of the Church; the four years that followed were spent in strife and doubts, and the last fourteen years in open schism. Though three of his children ascended the throne in succession, yet not one of them ever raised a monument to his memory. Mary, it is true, wished to do so, but her piety stood in the way, for she could not, being a Catholic, hand on to future generations the name of one who went into schism. Edward and Elizabeth, too, who approved of Henry's apostasy and schism, seem in this matter to have put away from themselves every sense of dutiful affection, unless it be that all this came to pass by the just judgment of God, that a man who scattered to the winds the ashes of so many saints, and who plundered the shrines of so many martyrs, should lie himself unhonoured in his grave.

ARBITER OF CHRISTENDOM

EDWARD HERBERT,
FIRST BARON HERBERT OF CHERBURY

This philosopher, historian, and diplomat was born in 1583. Educated at University College, Oxford, he was an accomplished courtier and traveler who won a reputation as a duelist long before he earned fame as a writer. After long service in France, Cherbury (an Irish peer) was a royalist and as such was put in the Tower in 1642; obtaining his release after an apology for a pro-royalist speech, he pursued a neutralist course in the Civil War. His French connections included Causabon and Gassendi among the intellectuals, and it is likely that they influenced his philosophical *De Veritate*, though not his *Autobiography*, which hardly touches his serious interests. Selden, his literary executor, published the apologetic *Life of Henry VIII* two years after Herbert's death, in 1649.

AND NOW if the reader (according to my manner in other great personages) do expect some character of this prince, I must affirm (as in the beginning) that the course of his life being commonly held various and diverse from it self, he will hardly suffer any, and that his history will be his best character and description.[1] Howbeit, since others have so much defam'd him, as will appear by the following objections, I shall strive to rectify their understandings who are impartial lovers of truth; without either presuming audaciously to condemn a prince, heretofore sovereign of our kingdom, or omitting the just freedom of an historian.

And because his most bitter censurers agree, that he had all manner of perfection, either of nature or education; and that he was (besides) of a most deep judgment in all affairs to which he apply'd himself; a prince not only liberal and indulgent to his family and court, but even to strangers, whom he willingly saw; and one that made choice both of able and good men for the clergy, and of wise and grave counsellors for his state-affairs; and above all, a prince of a royal courage: I shall not controvert these points, but come to my particular observations. According to which, I find him to have been ever most zealous of his honour and dignity; insomuch, that his most question'd passages were countenanc'd either with home or foreign authority: so many universities of Italy and France maintaining his repudiating of Queen Katharine of Spain; and his parliament (for the rest) authorizing the divorces and decapitations of his following wives, the dissolutions of the monasteries, and divers others of his most branded actions: so that by his parliaments in publick, and juries in private affairs, he at least wanted not colour and pretext to make them specious to the world; which also he had reason to affect: outward esteem and reputation being the same to great persons which the skin is to the fruit, which though it be but a slight and delicate cover, yet without it the fruit will presently discolour and rot.

[1] By "character" Herbert means here the sum of the mental and moral qualities which distinguish an individual. The writing of such "characters" was a seventeenth-century prose genre.

From Edward Herbert, *Autobiography of Edward, lord Herbert of Cherbury — the History of England under Henry VIII.* (London, 1870), pp. 743–48.

As for matter of state, I dare say, never prince went upon a truer maxim for this kingdom; which was, to make himself arbiter of Christendom: and had it not cost him so much, none had ever proceeded more wisely. But as he would be an actor (for the most part) where he needed only be a spectator, he both engaged himself beyond what was requisite, and by calling in the money he lent his confederates and allies, did often disoblige them when he had most need of their friendship. Yet thus he was the most active prince of his time. The examples whereof are so frequent in this history, that there was no treaty, or almost conventicle in Christendom, wherein he had not his particular agent and interest; which, together with his intelligence in all countries, and concerning all affairs, and the pensions given for that purpose, was one of his vast ways for spending of money.

Again, I observe, that there never was prince more delighted in interviews, or (generally) came off better from them. To which also, as his goodly personage and excellent qualities did much dispose him, so they gave him a particular advantage and lustre. Howbeit, as these voyages were extreme costly, so when he made use thereof to conclude a treaty, it did not always succeed; especially where credit was yielded to any single and private word. . . .

At home it was his manner to treat much with his parliaments; where, if gentle means serv'd not, he came to some degrees of the rough; though the more sparingly, in that he knew his people did but too much fear him. Besides, he understood well, that foul ways are not always passable, nor to be used (especially in suspected and dangerous times) but where others fail. However, it may be noted, that none of his predecessors understood the temper of parliaments better than himself, or that prevail'd himself more dexterously of them. Therefore, without being much troubled at the tumultuous beginnings of the rasher sort, he would give them that leave, which all new things must have, to settle. Which being done, his next care was to discover and prevent those privy combinations that were not for his service. After which, coming to the point of contribution,[2] he generally took strict order (by his commissioners) that gentlemen in the country should not spare each other; but that the true or (at least) near approaching value of every man's goods and lands should be certified. And this he did the rather, because he knew the custom of his people was to reckon with him about their subsidies, and indeed, rather to number, than to weigh their gifts.

As for his faults, I find that of opinionate and wilful much objected: insomuch, that the impressions privately given him by any court-whisperer, were hardly or never to be effaced. And herein the persons near him had a singular ability; while beginning with the commendations of those they would disgrace, their manner was to insinuate such exceptions, as they would discommend a man more in few words, than commend him in many: doing therein like cunning wrestlers, who to throw one down, first take him up. Besides, this wilfulness had a most dangerous quality annexed to it (especially towards his latter end) being an intense jealousy almost of all persons and affairs, which disposed him easily to think the worst. Whereas it is a greater part of wisdom to prevent, than to suspect. These conditions again being armed with power, produc'd such terrible effects, as stiled him both at home and abroad by the name of cruel; which also hardly can be avoided; especially, if that attribute be due, not only to those princes who inflict capital punishments frequently, and for small crimes, but to those who pardon not all that are capable of mercy. And for testimonies in this kind, some urge two queens, one cardinal . . . or two, (for Poole was condemn'd, tho' absent)[3] dukes, marquisses,

[2] Taxes levied by parliamentary grant or other direct impositions. The "subsidies" were one variety of such taxes and were levied either on land or fixed capital (personalty).

[3] Reginald Pole, the King's cousin, with whom Henry broke over the Divorce and Supremacy, Pole then accepting a cardinal's hat from Rome.

earls, and earls sons, twelve; barons and knights, eighteen; abbots, priors, monks and priests, seventy seven; of the more common sort, between one religion and another, huge multitudes.[4] He gave some proofs yet that he could forgive; tho' as they were few and late, they serv'd not to recover him the name of a clement prince. As for covetousness, or rapine, another main fault observ'd by Sanders, as extending not only to a promiscuous overthrow of religious houses, but a notable derogation of title of supreme head of the Church in his dominions, (and the rather, that he still retained the substance of the Roman Catholick religion) nothing, that I know, can on those terms palliate it, unless it might be collected, that the religious orders in his kingdom would have assisted those who threaten'd invasion from abroad, and that he had no other extraordinary means than their revenues then left to defend himself. For certainly, the publick pretext, taken from their excessive numbers in proportion to a well-compos'd state, or the inordinate and vicious life of the general sort, cannot sufficiently excuse him; since, together with the supernumerary and debauch'd abbeys, priories and nunneries, he subverted and extinguished the good and opportune; without leaving any receptacle for such as through age or infirmity being unapt for secular business, would end their days in a devout and a retir'd life. Nevertheless, as he erected divers new bishopricks, increased the number of colleges, and the stipend of readers in the universities, and did many other pious works, it is probable he intended some reparation. Tho' (as the Roman Catholick party conceives it) they were neither satisfactory for, nor equivalent to the desolations and ruins he procur'd, when yet he should pretend that the revenues and number of the gentry and soldatesque of the kingdom were augmented thereby. Howbeit, as in this act of overthrowing monasteries, his parliaments were

4 Recent researches of G. R. Elton have proved that only a little more than 300 of about 800 indicted for treason were convicted.

deeply engag'd, it will be dangerous to question the authority thereof, since things done by publick vote, where they find not reason, make it; neither have many laws other ground than the constitution of the times; which yet afterwards changing, leave their interpretation doubtful: insomuch, that posterity might justly abrogate them when the causes thereof ceas'd, had they the power to do it. For which regard also I shall not interpose my opinion otherwise, than that this king had met with no occasion to do that which hath caused so much scandal to him and his parliaments.

But whereas Sanders hath remarked covetousness as a great vice in this king, I could wish it had been with more limitation, and so as he noted the other extreme (being prodigality) for the greater fault: the examples of both being so pregnant in the king's father and himself. The first, by an exact inquiry into the corruptions and abuses of his officers and subjects, and the prevailing himself thereof to bring all into good order; and the getting of money together, whether by ordinary or extraordinary means (only when they were not manifestly unjust) and lastly, by frugality, acquiring to himself the name of prudent at home, and puissant abroad; as being known to have in his coffers always as much as would pay an army royal. Whereas this king, so often exhausting his treasury, that he was constrain'd at last to have recourse to unusual and grievous ways for relieving his wants, did not only disaffect his subjects in great part (as appear'd in the rebellion of the northern men and others, tho' to their confusion) but expos'd his kingdom to the invasion of his neighbours: who knowing (as all princes do) to about how much their neighbours revenues amount, and that there remain'd no longer any ready way to improve them, did collect thence what forces he could furnish; and consequently, would have assail'd him at home, but that their mutual divisions did hinder them. Whereby it appears, that what in Henry VII is call'd by some covetousness, was a royal vertue: whereas the excessive and needless expences of Henry VIII drew after them those miserable consequences which the world hath so much reproach'd. Howbeit, there may be occasion to doubt, whether the immense treasure which Henry VII left behind, were not (accidentally) the cause of those ills that follow'd: while the young prince his son, finding such a mass of money, did first carelessly spend, and after strive to supply as he could.

As for the third vice, wherewith he was justly charg'd, being lust and wantonness; there is *little to answer*, more than it was rather a personal fault, than damageable to the publick: howbeit, they who reprove it, ought not only to examine circumstances (which much aggravate and extenuate the fact) but even the complexions of men. It doth not yet appear that this fault did hasten the death of his queens; he being noted more for practising of private pleasures, than secret mischiefs; so that if any undue motive did co-operate herein, it may be thought an inordinate desire to have posterity (especially masculine) which might be the undoubted heirs of him and the kingdom, rather than any thing else.

With all his crimes, yet he was one of the most glorious princes of his time: insomuch, that not only the chief potentates of Christendom did court him, but his subjects in general did highly reverence him, as the many tryals he put them to, sufficiently testifie: which yet expir'd so quickly, that it may be truly said, all his pomp died with him; his memory being now expos'd to that obloquy, as his accusers will neither admit reason of state to cover any where, or necessity to excuse his actions. For, as they were either discontented clergymen (for his relinquishing the papal authority, and overthrowing the monasteries;) or offended women (for divers severe examples against their sex) that first oppos'd and cry'd him down, the clamour hath been the greater: so that although one William Thomas a clerk to the council to Edward the Sixth, and living about the latter times of Henry the Eighth's reign, did in great part defend him in an Italian book, printed anno 1552, it hath not avail'd.[5]

But what this prince was, and whether, and how far forth excusable in point of state, conscience, or honour, a diligent observation of his actions, together with a conjuncture of the times, will (I conceive) better declare to the judicious reader, than any factious relation on what side whatsoever. To conclude; I wish I could leave Henry VIII in his grave.

[5] The defense of Henry VIII by Thomas was a generous act; the author was compelled to flee England in 1544 on account of his heretical and radical opinions.

THE SCOURGE OF POPERY

BISHOP GILBERT BURNET

This son of a wealthy Edinburgh lawyer (1643–1715) studied in Marischal College, Aberdeen, where his special interests were in divinity, law, and history. While still a young man he also studied at Paris and Amsterdam. His divinity was such that he thrice refused the Covenant and in the 1660's favored a mild ecclesiastical policy at court. In 1669, after various services to Charles II's government, he received a professorship in divinity in Glasgow. By 1670 he was again engaged in the court politics of religion. He was not among the persecutors of Roman Catholics. Amidst such cares and after being dismissed as a royal chaplain, thoroughly disliked by the courtiers and the extreme antipapal factions, Burnet began his monumental *History of the Reformation of the Church of England.* From that time (1679) until his death politics and composition were his preoccupations, a fact which informs his *History of His Own Time* as well as many sermons and pamphlets.

A$_{ND NOW}$ having ended what I have to say of king Henry, I will add a few reflections on him and on his reign. He had certainly a greater measure of knowledge in learning, more particularly in divinity, than most princes of that or of any age: that gave occasion to those excessive flatteries, which in a great measure corrupted his temper, and disfigured his whole government. It is deeply rooted in the nature of man to love to be flattered, because self-love makes men their own flatterers, and so they do too easily take down the flatteries that are offered them by others; who, when they expect advantages by it, are too ready to give this incense to their vanity, according to the returns that they expect from it.

Few are so honest and disinterested in their friendship as to consider the real good of others, but choose rather to comply with their humour and vanity: and since princes have most to give, flattery (too common to all places) is the natural growth of courts; in which, if there are some few so unfashioned to those places as to seek the real good and honour of the prince by the plain methods of blunt honesty, which may carry them to contradict a mistaken prince, to shew him his errors, and with a true firmness of courage to try to work even against the grain; while they pursue that, which, though it is the real advantage and honour of the prince, yet it is not agreeable to some weak or perverse humour in him; these are soon overtopped by a multitude of flatterers, who will find it an easy work to undermine such faithful ministers, because their own candour and fidelity makes them use none of the arts of a countermine. Thus the flattered prince easily goes into the hands of those who humour and please him most, without regarding either the true honour of the master or the good of the community.

If weak princes, of a small measure of knowledge, and a low capacity, fall into such hands, the government will dwindle into an unactive languishing; which will make them a prey to all about them, and expose them to universal contempt both at home and abroad: while the flatterers make

From Gilbert Burnet, *The History of the Reformation of the Church of England* (Oxford, England, 1865), III, pp. 298–303. Reprinted by permission of The Clarendon Press, Oxford.

their own advantages and chief measure of the government, and do so besiege the abused and deluded prince, that he fancies he is the wonder and delight of all the world, when he is under the last degrees of the scorn of the worst, and of the pity of the best of his people.

But if these flatterers gain the ascendant over princes of genius and capacity, they put them on great designs, under the false representations of conquests and glory; they engage them either to make or break leagues at pleasure, to enter upon hostilities without any previous steps or declarations of war, to ruin their own people for supporting those wars that are carried on with all the methods both of barbarity and perfidy: while a studied luxury and vanity at home is kept up, to amuse and blind the ignorant beholders with a false show of lustre and magnificence.

This had too deep a root in king Henry, and was too long flattered by cardinal Wolsey, to be ever afterwards brought into due bounds and just measures; yet Wolsey pursued the true maxims of England, of maintaining the balance during his ministry.[1] Our trade lay then so entirely in the Netherlands, without our seeming to think to carry it farther, that it was necessary to maintain a good correspondence with those provinces; and Charles' dominions were so widely scattered, that, till Francis was taken prisoner, it was visibly the interest of England to continue still jealous of France, and to favour Charles. But the taking of Francis the First changed the scene; France was then to be supported; it was also so exhausted, and Charles' revenue was so increased, that, without great sums both lent him and expended by England, all must have sunk under Charles' power, if England had not held the balance.

It was also a masterpiece in Wolsey to engage the king to own that the book

against Luther was written by him, in which the secret of those who, no doubt, had the greatest share in composing it was so closely laid, that it never broke out. Seckendorf tells us, that Luther believed it was writ by Lee,[2] who was a zealous Thomist, and had been engaged in disputes with Erasmus, and was afterwards made archbishop of York. If any of those who still adhered to the old doctrines had been concerned in writing it, probably, when they saw king Henry depart from so many points treated of in it, they would have gone beyond sea, and have robbed him of that false honour and those excessive praises which that book had procured him. It is plain More wrote it not: for the king having shewed it him before it was published, he (as he mentions in one of his letters to Cromwell) told the king, that he had raised the papacy so high, that it might be objected to him, if he should happen to have any dispute with the pope, as was often between princes and popes; and it will be found in the remarks on the former volumes, that he in another letter says, he was a *sorter* of that book. This seems to relate only to the digesting it into method and order.

How far king Henry was sincere in pretending scruples of conscience with relation to his first marriage, can only be known to God. His suit of divorce was managed at a vast expense, in a course of many years; in all which time, how strong soever his passion was for Anne Boleyn, yet her being with child so soon after their marriage was a clear evidence that till then they had no unlawful commerce. It does not appear that Wolsey deserved his disgrace, unless it was, that by the commission given to the two legates they were empowered to act conjunctly or severally; so that, though Campeggio refused to concur, he might have given sentence legally; yet he being trusted by the pope, his acting according to instructions did not deserve so severe a correction: and had any material discovery

---

[1] That Wolsey's diplomacy rested on the axiom "balance of powers" cannot be maintained; as both Pollard and Garrett Mattingly have demonstrated, Wolsey's policies contributed to the imperial victory over the Valois.

[2] Edward Lee.

been made to render Wolsey criminal, it may be reasonably supposed it would have been published.

The new flatterers falling in with the king's passion outdid and ruined Wolsey. More was the glory of the age; and his advancement was the king's honour more than his own, who was a true Christian philosopher.[3] He thought the cause of the king's divorce was just, and as long as it was prosecuted at the court of Rome, so long he favoured it: but when he saw that a breach with that court was like to follow, he left the great post he was in with a superior greatness of mind. It was a fall great enough to retire from that into a private state of life: but the carrying matters so far against him as the king did, was one of the justest reproaches of that reign. More's superstition seems indeed contemptible; but the constancy of his mind was truly wonderful.

Cromwell's ministry was in a constant course of flattery and submission; but by that he did great things, that amaze one who has considered them well. The setting up the king's supremacy instead of the usurpations of the papacy, and the rooting out the monastic state in England, considering the wealth, the numbers, and the zeal of the monks and friars in all the parts of the kingdom, as it was a very bold undertaking, so it was executed with great method, and performed in so short a time, and with so few of the convulsions that might have been expected, that all this shews what a master he was, that could bring such a design to be finished in so few years, with so little trouble or danger.

But in conclusion, an unfortunate marriage, to which he advised the king, not proving acceptable, and he being unwilling to destroy what he himself had brought about, was no doubt backward in the design of breaking it, when the king had told him of it: and then, upon no other visible ground but because Anne of Cleves grew more obliging to the king than she was

[3] Burnet's remarks about counsel and flattery echo More's in *Utopia*, Book I.

formerly, the king suspected that Cromwell had betrayed his secret, and had engaged her to a softer deportment on design to prevent the divorce; and did upon that, disgrace and destroy him.

The duke of Norfolk was never till Cromwell's fall the first in favour; but he had still kept his post by perpetual submission and flattery. He was sacrificed at last to the king's jealousy, fearing that he might be too great in his son's infancy; and, being considered as the head of the popish party, might engage in an easy competition with the Seymours during the minority of his son: for the points he was at first examined on were of an old date, of no consequence, and supported by no proof.

When the king first threw off the pope's yoke, the reformers offered him in their turn all the flatteries they could decently give: and if they could have had the patience to go no further than as he was willing to parcel out a reformation to them, he had perhaps gone further in it. But he seemed to think, that as it was pretended in popery, that infallibility was to go along with the supremacy, therefore those who had yielded the one ought likewise to submit to the other; he turned against them when he saw that their complaisance did not go so far. And upon that, the adherers to the old opinions returned to their old flatteries, and for some time seemed to have brought him quite back to them: which probably might have wrought more powerfully, but that he found the old leaven of the papacy was still working in them. So that he was all the while fluctuating: sometimes making steps to a reformation, but then returning back to his old notions. One thing probably wrought much on him. It has appeared, that he had great apprehensions of the council that was to meet at Trent, and that the emperor's engagements to restrain the council from proceeding in his matter was the main article of the new friendship made up between them: and it may be very reasonably supposed, that the emperor represented to him, that nothing could secure that matter so certainly as his not proceeding to any further innovations in religion; more particularly his adhering firmly to the received doctrine of Christ's presence in the sacrament, and the other article set forth by him. This agreeing with his own opinion, had, as may be well imagined, no small share in the change of his conduct at that time.

The dextrous application of flattery had generally a powerful effect on him: but whatsoever he was, and how great soever his pride and vanity and his other faults were, he was a great instrument in the hand of Providence for many good ends: he first opened the door to let light in upon the nation; he delivered it from the yoke of blind and implicit obedience; he put the scriptures in the hands of the people, and took away the terror they were formerly under by the cruelty of the ecclesiastical courts; he declared this church to be an entire and perfect body within itself, with full authority to decree and to regulate all things, without any dependence on any foreign power; and he did so unite the supreme headship over this church to the imperial crown of this realm, that it seemed a just consequence that was made by some in a popish reign, that he who would not own that this supremacy was in him, did by that renounce the crown, of which that title was made so essential a part, that they could no more be separated.

He attacked popery in its strong holds the monasteries, and destroyed them all: and thus he opened the way to all that came after, even down to our days. So that, while we see the folly and weakness of man in all his personal failings, which were very many and very enormous; we at the same time see both the justice, the wisdom, and the goodness of God, in making him, who was once the pride and glory of popery, become its scourge and destruction; and in directing his pride and passion so as to bring about, under the dread of his unrelenting temper, a change that a milder reign could not have compassed without great convulsions and much confusion: above all the rest, we ought to adore the goodness of God in rescuing us by his means from idolatry and superstition: from the vain and pompous shows in which the worship of God was dressed up, so as to vie with heathenism itself, into a simplicity of believing, and a purity of worship, conform to the nature and attributes of God, and the doctrine and example of the Son of God.

May we ever value this as we ought; and may we in our tempers and lives so express the beauty of this holy religion, that it may ever shine among us, and may shine out from us, to all round about us: and then we may hope that God will preserve it to us, and to posterity after us, for ever!

THE IMAGE OF GOD UPON EARTH

JOHN LINGARD

An English Roman Catholic, John Lingard was born in 1771; as a young boy he went abroad to study in Douay (1782–1793) and returned home a priest. His genius was for writing and research and it showed itself by 1806, when *The Antiquities of the Anglo-Saxon Church* appeared. Thereafter dividing his energies between his historical pursuits and Roman business in England, Lingard worked steadily on his great *History* from 1811 to 1830. The book was immensely popular and saw five editions before his death in 1851.

WE MAY NOW return to the defunct monarch. To form a just estimate of the character of Henry, we must distinguish between the young king, guided by the counsels of Wolsey, and the monarch of more mature age, governing by his own judgment, and with the aid of ministers selected and fashioned by himself. In his youth, the beauty of his person, the elegance of his manners, and his adroitness in every martial and fashionable exercise, were calculated to attract the admiration of his subjects. His court was gay and splendid; and a succession of amusements seemed to absorb his attention; yet his pleasures were not permitted to encroach on his more important duties; he assisted at the council, perused the despatches, and corresponded with his generals and ambassadors; nor did the minister, trusted and powerful as he was, dare to act, till he had asked the opinion, and taken the pleasure of his sovereign. His natural abilities had been improved by study; and his esteem for literature may be inferred from the learned education which he gave to his children, and from the number of eminent scholars to whom he granted pensions in foreign states, or on whom he bestowed preferment in his own. The immense treasure which he inherited from his father was perhaps a misfortune; because it engendered habits of expense not to be supported from the ordinary revenue of the crown; and the soundness of his politics may be doubted, which, under the pretence of supporting the balance of power, repeatedly involved the nation in continental hostilities. Yet even these errors served to throw a lustre round the English throne, and raised its possessor in the eyes of his own subjects and of the different nations of Europe. But as the king advanced in age, his vices gradually developed themselves; after the death of Wolsey they were indulged without restraint. He became as rapacious as he was prodigal; as obstinate as he was capricious; as fickle in his friendships, as he was merciless in his resentments. Though liberal of his confidence, he soon grew suspicious of those whom he had trusted; and, as if he possessed no other right to the crown than that which he derived from the very questionable claim of his father, he viewed with an evil eye every remote descendant of the Plantagenets; and eagerly embraced the slightest pretexts to remove those whom his jealousy represented as future rivals to himself or his posterity. In pride and vanity he was perhaps without a parallel. Inflated with the praises of interested admirers, he despised

From John Lingard, *The History of England from the First Invasion by the Romans to the Accession of William and Mary in 1688* (London, 1855), IV, pp. 107–13.

the judgment of others; acted as if he deemed himself infallible in matters of policy and religion; and seemed to look upon dissent from his opinion as equivalent to a breach of allegiance. In his estimation, to submit and obey were the great, the paramount duties of subjects; and this persuasion steeled his breast against remorse for the blood which he shed, and led him to trample without scruple on the liberties of the nation.

When he ascended the throne, there still existed a spirit of freedom, which on more than one occasion defeated the arbitrary measures of the court, though directed by an able minister, and supported by the authority of sovereign; but in the lapse of a few years that spirit had fled, and before the death of Henry, the king of England had grown into a despot, the people had shrunk into a nation of slaves. The causes of this important change in the relations between the sovereign and his subjects, may be found not so much in the abilities or passions of the former, as in the obsequiousness of his parliaments, his assumption of the ecclesiastical supremacy, and the servility of the two religious parties which divided the nation.

I. The house of Peers no longer consisted of those powerful lords and prelates, who in former periods had so often and so successfully resisted the encroachments of the sovereign. The reader has already witnessed the successive steps by which most of the great families of the preceding reigns had become extinct, and their immense possessions had been frittered away among the favourites and dependants of the court. The most opulent of the peers under Henry were poor in comparison with their predecessors; and by the operation of the statute against liveries, they had lost the accustomed means of arming their retainers in support of their quarrels. In general they were new men, indebted for their present honours and estates to the bounty of Henry or of his father; and the proudest among the rest, by witnessing the attainders and executions of others, had been taught to tremble for themselves, and to crouch in submission at the foot of a master, whose policy it was to depress the great, and punish their errors without mercy, while he selected his favourites from the lowest classes, heaping on them honours and riches, and confiding to them the exercise of his authority.

2. By the separation of the realm from the see of Rome, the dependence of the spiritual had been rendered still more complete than that of the temporal peers. Their riches had been diminished, their immunities taken away; the support which they might have derived from the protection of the pontiff was gone; they were nothing more than the delegates of the king, exercising a precarious authority determinable at his pleasure. The ecclesiastical constitutions, which had so long formed part of the law of the land, now depended on his breath, and were executed only by his sufferance. The convocation indeed continued to be summoned; but its legislative authority was gone. Its principal business was to grant money; yet even these grants now owed their force, not to the consent of the grantors, but to the approbation of the other two houses, and the assent of the crown.

3. As for the third branch of the legislature, the Commons of England, they had not yet acquired sufficient importance to oppose any effectual barrier to the power of the sovereign; yet care was taken that among them the leading members should be devoted to the crown, and that the speaker should be one holding office, or high in the confidence of the ministers. Freedom of debate was, indeed, granted; but with a qualification which in reality amounted to a refusal. It was only a *decent* freedom; and as the king reserved to himself the right of deciding what was or was not decent, he frequently put down the opponents of the court, by reprimanding the "varlets" in person, or by sending to them a threatening message.

It is plain that from parliaments thus constituted, the crown had little to fear;

and though Wolsey had sought to govern without their aid, Henry found them so obsequious to his will, that he convoked them repeatedly, and was careful to have his most wanton and despotic measures sanctioned with their approbation. The parliament, as often as it was opened or closed by the king in person, offered a scene not unworthy of an oriental divan. The form indeed differed but little from our present usage. The king sat on this throne; on the right hand stood the chancellor, on the left the lord treasurer; whilst the peers were placed on their benches, and the commons stood at the bar. But the addresses made on these occasions by the chancellor or the speaker, usually lasted more than an hour; and their constant theme was the character of the king. The orators, in their efforts to surpass each other, fed his vanity with the most hyperbolical praise. Cromwell was unable, he believed all men were unable, to describe the unutterable qualities of the royal mind, the sublime virtues of the royal heart. Rich[1] told him that in wisdom he was equal to Solomon, in strength and courage to Sampson, in beauty and address to Absalom; and Audley[2] declared before his face, that God had anointed him with the oil of wisdom above his fellows, above the other kings of the earth, above all his predecessors; had given him a perfect knowledge of the Scriptures, with which he had prostrated the Roman Goliath; a perfect knowledge of the art of war, by which he had gained the most brilliant victories at the same time in remote places; and a perfect knowledge of the art of government, by which he had for thirty years secured to his own realm the blessings of peace, while all the other nations of Europe suffered the calamities of war.

During these harangues, as often as the words "most sacred majesty" were repeated, or any emphatic expression was pronounced, the lords rose, and the whole assembly, in token of respect and assent, bowed profoundly to the demigod on the throne. Henry himself affected to hear such fulsome adulation with indifference. His answer was invariably the same; that he had no claim to superior excellence; but that, if he did possess it, he gave the glory to God, the Author of all good gifts; it was, however, a pleasure to him to witness the affection of his subjects, and to learn that they were not insensible of the blessings which they enjoyed under his government.

II. It is evident that the new dignity of head of the church, by transferring to the king that authority which had been hitherto exercised by the pontiff, must have considerably augmented the influence of the crown; but in addition, the arguments by which it was supported tended to debase the spirit of the people, and to exalt the royal prerogative above law and equity. When the adversaries of the supremacy asked in what passage of the sacred writings the government of the church was given to a layman, its advocates boldly appealed to those texts which precribe obedience to the established authorities.[3] The king, they maintained, was the image of God upon earth; to disobey his commands was to disobey God himself; to limit his authority, when no limit was laid down, was an offence against the sovereign; and to make distinctions, when the Scripture made none, was an impiety against God. It was indeed acknowledged that this supreme authority might be employed unreasonably and unjustly; but even then to resist was a crime; it became the duty of the sufferer to submit; and his only resource was to pray that the heart of his oppressor might be changed; his only consolation to reflect, that the king himself would hereafter be summoned to answer for his conduct before an unerring tribunal. Henry became a sincere believer in a doctrine so flattering to his pride, and easily persuaded himself

[1] Sir Richard Rich, Attorney-General, Chancellor of Augmentations, later Lord Chancellor of England, and the man whose testimony, probably perjured, sent More to his martyrdom.

[2] Thomas Lord Audley, a lawyer and politician of Cromwell's circle; he was Lord Chancellor from 1532 to 1544.

[3] *Romans*, I, 13: "Render unto Caesar . . ." and various places in Corinthians.

that he did no more than his duty in punishing with severity the least opposition to his will. To impress it on the minds of the people, it was perpetually inculcated from the pulpit; it was enforced in books of controversy and instruction; it was promulgated with authority in the "Institution" and afterwards in the "Erudition of a Christian Man." From that period the doctrine of passive obedience formed a leading trait in the orthodox creed.

III. The two great parties into which religious disputes had divided the nation, contributed also to strengthen the despotic power of Henry. They were too jealous of each other to watch, much less to resist, the encroachments of the crown. The great object of both was the same; to win the favour of the king, that they might crush the power of their adversaries; and with this view they flattered his vanity, submitted to his caprice, and became obsequious slaves to his pleasure. Henry, on the other hand, whether it were through policy or accident, played them off against each other; sometimes appearing to lean to the old, sometimes to the new doctrines, alternately raising and depressing the hopes of each, but never suffering either party to obtain the complete ascendancy over its opponent. Thus he kept them in a state of dependence on his will, and secured their concurrence to every measure which his passion or caprice might suggest, without regard to reason or justice, or the fundamental laws of the land. Of the extraordinary enactments which followed, a few instances may suffice. 1. The succession to the crown was repeatedly altered, and at length left to the king's private judgment or affection. The right was first taken from Mary, and given to Elizabeth; then transferred from Elizabeth to the king's issue by Jane Seymour or any future queen; next restored, on the failure of issue by Prince Edward, to both Mary and Elizabeth; and lastly, failing issue by them, entailed upon any person or persons to whom it should please him to assure it in remainder by his last will. 2. Treasons were multiplied by the most vexatious, and often, if ridicule could attach to so grave a matter, by the most ridiculous laws. It was once treason to dispute, it was afterwards treason to maintain, the validity of the marriage with Anne Boleyn, or the legitimacy of her daughter. It became treason to marry, without the royal license, any of the king's children, whether legitimate or natural, or his paternal brothers or sisters, or their issue; or for any woman to marry the king himself, unless she were a maid, or had previously revealed to him her former incontinence. It was made treason to call the king a heretic or schismatic, openly to wish him harm, or to slander him, his wife, or his issue. This, the most heinous of crimes in the eye of the law, was extended from deeds and assertions to the very thoughts of men. Its guilt was incurred by any person who should, by words, writing, imprinting, or any other exterior act, directly or indirectly accept or take, judge or believe, that either of the royal marriages, that with Catherine, or that with Anne Boleyn, was valid, or who should protest that he was not bound to declare his opinion, or should refuse to swear that he would answer truly such questions as should be asked him on those dangerous subjects. It would be difficult to discover, under the most despotic governments, a law more cruel and absurd. The validity or invalidity of the two marriages was certainly matter of opinion, supported and opposed on each side by so many contradictory arguments, that men of the soundest judgment might reasonably be expected to differ from each other. Yet Henry, by this statute, was authorized to dive into the breast of every individual, to extort from him his secret sentiments upon oath, and to subject him to the penalty of treason, if those sentiments did not accord with the royal pleasure. 3. The king was made in a great measure independent of parliament, by two statutes, one of which put his proclamations on the same footing with acts of parliament,[4] provided they did not set aside laws

[4] G. R. Elton has shown this view of the Act of Proclamations to be in error. Far from being an instrument of despotism, the 1539 act reinforced the conservatism of common law.

actually in force, nor enjoin the penalties of disherison or death in any cases but those of heretical doctrine; the other appointed a tribunal, consisting of nine privy counsellors, with power to punish all transgressors of such proclamations. 4. The dreadful punishment of heresy was not confined to those who rejected the doctrines which had already been declared orthodox, but it was extended beforehand to all persons who should teach or maintain any opinion contrary to such doctrines as the king might afterwards publish. If the criminal were a clergyman, he was to expiate his third offence at the stake; if a layman, to forfeit his personal property, and be imprisoned for life. Thus was Henry invested, by act of parliament, with the high prerogative of theological infallibility, and an obligation was laid on all men, without exception, whether of the new or of the old learning, to model their religious opinions and religious practice by the sole judgment of their sovereign. 5. By an ex post facto law, those who had taken the first oath against the papal authority, were reputed to have taken, and to be bound by, a second and much more comprehensive oath, which was afterwards enacted, and which, perhaps, had it been tendered to them at first, they would have refused.

But that which made the severity of these statutes the more terrible, was the manner in which criminal prosecutions were then conducted. The crown could hardly fail in convicting the prisoner, whatever might be his guilt or his innocence. He was first interrogated in his cell, urged with the hope of pardon to make a confession, or artfully led by ensnaring questions into dangerous admissions. When the materials of the prosecution were completed, they were laid before the grand inquest; and, if the bill was found, the conviction of the accused might be pronounced certain; for, in the trial which followed, the real question submitted to the decision of the petit jury was, which of the two were more worthy of credit — the prisoner who maintained his innocence, or the grand inquest which had pronounced his guilt.

With this view the indictment, with a summary of the proofs on which it had been found, was read; and the accused, now perhaps for the first time acquainted with the nature of the evidence against him, was indulged with the liberty of speaking in his own defence. Still he could not insist on the production of his accusers, that he might obtain the benefit of cross-examination; nor claim the aid of counsel to repel the taunts, and unravel the sophistry, too often employed at that period by the advocates of the crown. In this method of trial, every chance was in favour of the prosecution; and yet it was gladly exchanged for the expedient discovered by Cromwell, and afterward employed against its author. Instead of a public trial, the minister introduced a bill of attainder into parliament, accompanied with such documents as he thought proper to submit. It was passed by the two houses with all convenient expedition; and the unfortunate prisoner found himself condemned to the scaffold or the gallows, without the opportunity of opening his mouth in his own vindication.[5]

To proceed by attainder became the usual practice in the latter portion of the king's reign. It was more certain in the result, by depriving the accused of the few advantages which he possessed in the ordinary courts; it enabled the minister to gratify the royal suspicion or resentment without the danger of refutation, or of unpleasant disclosures; and it satisfied the minds of the people, who, unacquainted with the real merits of the case, could not dispute the equity of a judgment given with the unanimous assent of the whole legislature.

Thus it was that by the obsequiousness of the parliament, the assumption of the ecclesiastical supremacy, and the servility of religious factions, Henry acquired and

[5] This entire passage is seriously in error. With few exceptions, attainders were passed after conviction under common law trial in King's Bench or before itinerant judges commissioned in the normal manner. Also, as has been said before, the Crown often failed to get convictions, such was the rigor of its adherence to common law procedure in the 1530's.

exercised the most despotic sway over the lives, the fortunes, and the liberties of his subjects. Happily, the forms of a free government were still suffered to exist; into these forms a spirit of resistance to arbitrary power gradually infused itself; the pretensions of the crown were opposed by the claims of the people; and the result of a long and arduous struggle was that constitution which for more than a century has excited the envy and the admiration of Europe.

THE JUDGMENT UPON HIS MOTIVES AND ACTIONS

JAMES ANTHONY FROUDE

This historian's twelve volumes of English history from 1530 to 1588 are remarkable literary accomplishments. Froude's strong Protestantism, which caused him to stray from orthodoxy in his *Nemesis of Faith* in 1849, leaves its mark upon his characterization of Henry VIII. Educated at Oriel College, Oxford, he was an essayist, traveler, politician dabbling in the causes of South African federation, and above all else a historian. As Carlyle's chief disciple and literary executor alone he had a full career. Late in his life, from 1892 to 1894, he was Regius Professor in Oxford University, and it is upon his work there that such familiar books as *Life and Letters of Erasmus, English Seamen in the Sixteenth Century*, and *The Council of Trent* are based, all published posthumously.

TREMENDOUS as the outward overthrow must have seemed to those who remembered the old days, the inward changes were yet more momentous. A superstition which was but the counterpart of magic and witchcraft, which buried the Father of heaven and earth in the coffins of the saints, and trusted the salvation of the soul to the efficacy of mumbled words, had given place to a real, though indistinct, religion. Copies of the Bible were spread over the country in tens of thousands. Every English child was taught in its own tongue the Lord's Prayer, and the Creed, and the Commandments. Idolatry existed no longer; and the remaining difficulties lay only in the interpretation of the Sacred Text, and in the clinging sense, which adhered to all sides alike, that to misunderstand it was not an error, but a crime. Here, although Catholic doctrine, not only in its practical corruptions, but in its purest "developments," shook at the contact with the Gospels, yet the most thoughtful had been compelled to pause embarrassed. If mistake was fatal, and if the Divine nature and the Divine economy could not be subject to change, to reject the interpretations on which that doctrine had maintained itself, was to condemn the Christian Church to have been deserted for a thousand years by the spirit of truth, and this was a conclusion too frightful, too incredible to be endured. The laity, so bold against the Pope and the monasteries, turned their faces from it into the dogmatism of the Six Articles.[1]

Yet still the genius of change went onward, caring little for human opposition. To move with it, or to move against it, affected little the velocity with which the English world was swept into the New Era. The truth stole into men's minds they knew not how. The King, as we have seen, began to shrink from persecution, and to shelter suspected persons from orthodox cruelty. The Parliament, which would not yet alter the heresy law, tempered the action of it, and was rather contented to retard a movement which threatened to be

[1] The conservative statement of "necessary" doctrinal truths passed by Parliament in 1539.

From James A. Froude, *History of England, From the Fall of Wolsey to the Defeat of the Spanish Armada* (London, Longmans Green, n.d.), IV, pp. 186–95 and 236–43.

too wildly precipitate than attempt any more to arrest it.

Next to the Bible, there are few things which have affected the character of the modern English more deeply than the Liturgy. The beautiful roll of its language mingles with the memories of childhood; it is the guide of our dawning thought, and accompanies us through each stage of our life with its chaste ceremonials from the font to the edge of the grave. Having been composed at a period when old and new beliefs were contending for supremacy, it contains some remnants of opinions which have no longer perhaps a place in our convictions; but the more arduous problems of speculation are concealed behind a purposed vagueness which shrinks from definition; and the spirit of the Prayer Book is the spirit of piety more than of theology, of wisdom more than of dogma.

Thus, although as an historical document the Liturgy is valuable as a picture of the minds of the English Reformers, it is with a keener interest that we watch the first gems of it passing into the form with which we are so familiar. Two English primers had been published since the commencement of the movement, one in 1535, another under the auspices of Cromwell in 1539; but the first of these was passionate and polemical, the second was slightly altered from the Breviary. If we except the Creed, the Commandments, and the Lord's Prayer, which were attached to the articles of religion sent out in 1536, the earliest portion of our own Prayer Book which appeared in English was the Litany, prepared by the King in the summer of 1544, and perhaps translated by him. On the eve of his departure to Boulogne he sent it, with the following letter, to Cranmer, to be circulated through the country.

Right Reverend Father in God, right trusty and well beloved, we greet you well; and let you wit that, calling to our remembrance the miserable state of all Christendom, being at this present, besides all other troubles, so plagued with most cruel wars, hatreds, and dissensions, as no place of the same — almost being the whole reduced to a very narrow corner — remaineth in good peace and concord — the help and remedy hereof, far exceeding the power of any man, must be called for of Him who only is able to grant our petitions, and never forsaketh or repelleth any that firmly believe and faithfully call upon Him; unto whom also the examples of Scripture encourage us in all these and others our troubles and necessities to flee. Being therefore resolved to have continually, from henceforth, general processions in all cities, towns, churches, and parishes of this our realm, said and sung with such reverence and devotion as appertaineth, for as much as heretofore the people partly for lack of good instruction and calling, partly for that they understood no part of such prayers and suffrages as were used to be said and sung, have used to come very slackly to the processions, where the same have been commanded heretofore, we have set forth certain godly prayers and suffrages in our native English tongue, which we send you herewith; signifying unto you that, for the special trust and confidence we have of your godly mind and earnest desire to the setting forward of the glory of God and the true worshipping of his most holy name, within that province committed by us unto you, we have sent unto you these suffrages, not to be for a month or two observed and after slenderly considered, as our other injunctions have, to our no little marvel, been used; but to the intent, as well the same as other our injunctions, may earnestly be set forth by preaching, good exhortation, and otherwise, to the people, in such sort as they, feeling the godly taste thereof, may godly and joyously, with thanks, embrace the same as appertaineth.

In the year following a collection of English prayers was added to the Litany, a service for morning and evening, and for the burial of the dead; and the King, in a general proclamation, directed that they should be used in all churches and chapels in the place of the Breviary. It was the duty of the sovereign, he said, to endeavour that his subjects should pass their lives devoutly and virtuously, to the honour of God, and the salvation of their souls. Prayer was the appointed and the only means by which such a life was rendered possible; but prayer of the most passionate and ravishing kind was of little profit, if it was an emotion undirected by the understanding; and to make use of words in a foreign language, merely with a sentiment of devotion, the mind taking no fruit, could be neither pleasing to God, nor beneficial to man. The party that understood not the pith or effectualness of the talk that he made with God, might be as a harp or pipe, having a sound, but not understanding the noise that itself had made; a Christian man was more than an instrument; and he had therefore provided a determinate form of supplication in the English tongue, that his subjects might be able to pray like reasonable beings in their own language.

The surest testimony to wise and moderate measures is the disapproval of fanatics of all kinds. Amidst the factions which were raging around him, the King, with his rational advisers, had no desire to swell the clamour; he sought to accomplish something unquestionably genuine and good, which might bear fruit at a future time. But to the eager Protestants the prayers were tainted with Popery; falling short of their own extravagances they seemed as worthless as the Latin forms which they displaced: while the reactionaries, on the other hand, looked on with mere dismay, and watched for some change of fortune, or some fresh access of folly in their adversaries, to compel Henry once more to turn back upon his steps. As the moderate party was gaining ground, the discord between the extremes grew louder and more bitter; and in the midst of it Parliament met, after a longer interval than usual, in November 1545. From the "Statute Book" it would have appeared that the business of the session had been principally secular, or, at least, had touched but lightly on theological controversy. Fresh war taxes were voted. There were measures of law reform, and for the simplification of landed tenures. A remarkable Act stated that the laws of high treason had been made the instruments of private malice. Anonymous libels had been put in circulation, accusing innocent per-

sons of having used seditious language against the King; and, to prevent the multiplication of calumnies and suspicions, any person or persons who should have published any such charges, and not come forward in his own name to prove his statements in the Star Chamber, should in future suffer death as a felon. The Reformers obtained a victory in the dispensation from the vow of celibacy which was granted to the Knights of St. John. A commission was again appointed to revise the canon law; and married laymen were permitted to exercise jurisdiction in the ecclesiastical courts.

The dissolution of the monasteries had shaken the stability of all other religious or semi-religious corporations. Grants for religious uses, of whatever description, were no longer supposed to be permanent; and the founders, or the representatives of the founders, of colleges, hospitals, fraternities, brotherhoods, and guilds, had shown a disposition to resume their gifts. In some places the wardens or the occupiers had been expelled; in others sales had been effected by fraudulent collusion; in others the lands belonging to the foundations had been granted away in leases upon lives, the incumbents securing their personal interests by fines. Irregularities so considerable required interference, and, by a sweeping Act, all such properties were at once vested in the Crown, that the institutions to which they had belonged might be refounded on a fresh basis, if their continued existence was desirable. A momentary panic was created at Oxford and Cambridge, where the colleges expected the fate of the religious houses; and Doctor Coxe, the prince's tutor,[2] who was Dean of Christ Church, wrote, in some agitation, to Sir William Paget[3]: "Not," he said, "that I distrust the King's goodness, but because there are such a number of importunate wolves as are able

[2] Richard Coxe, Bishop of Ely, a liturgist and scholar who went into exile during Queen Mary's reign. He tutored Prince Edward.
[3] First Baron Paget of Beaudesert; diplomat, privy councillor, Secretary of State and Lord Privy Seal.

to devour chauntries, cathedral churches, universities, and a thousand times as much." The alarm was natural, but it was unnecessary. The King's object was rather to preserve and to restore than to destroy, and the scale and scope of his intentions were soon displayed so clearly as to dispel all uneasiness, by the foundation of the Hospital of St. Bartholomew, and of Trinity College at Cambridge.

*   *   *

But, as it would be affectation to seem to be unconscious that the character of the King, as presented in these volumes, is something different from that which modern tradition has ascribed to him, so for my own sake I desire to say that I have not advanced any novel paradox or conjectures of my own. The history of the reign of Henry VIII is a palimpsest in which the original writing can still be read; and I have endeavoured only to reinstate the judgment upon his motives and his actions — which was entertained by all moderate Englishmen in his own and the succeeding generation — which was displaced only by the calumnies of Catholic or Antinomian[4] fanatics, when the true records were out of sight; and when, in the establishment of a new order of things, the hesitating movements, the inconsistencies and difficulties, inevitable in a period of transition could no longer be understood without an effort.

The following passage, written by Ulpian Fulwell[5] early in the reign of Elizabeth, must be received with much qualification. From the language of contemporary panegyric later reflection must ever find something to detract; nor was the writer a person whose judgment is of exceptional or particular value. His words, nevertheless, may be taken to express the general admiration of the King's character which survived in the minds of the people.

[4] Literally, fanatics who are "against the law," that is, men who believed the law to be of no real importance, whether the law of Scripture or that of the body politic.

[5] Poet and chronicler, he flourished in the 1580's. His chief composition is *The Flower of Fame* (1575, a chronicle of Henry VIII).

Among the most fortunate kings and princes that ever reigned let the fortunes of King Henry VIII have a special place. This I may boldly say, that he was blest of God above all kings and princes that ever I have read of, and happy was that prince that might stand most in his favour; for the which divers made great suit, and especially when they stood in need of aid against their enemies, because they perceived that fortune followed his power as handmaid to all his proceedings. A rare example no doubt it is, and meseemeth most strange, that one king should reign thirty-eight years, and that almost in continual wars, and never take foil, but always prevailed as a victor invicted, which, without the assistance of Almighty God, he could never have achieved; an evident token that God was on his side, and therefore who could stand against him. To write at large of all his worthiness and incomparable acts would fill a volume, and were too great a charge. But he was a prince of singular prudence, of passing stout courage, of invincible fortitude, of dexterity wonderful. He was a springing well of eloquence, a rare spectacle of humanity; of civility and good nature an absolute precedent, a special pattern of clemency and moderation, a worthy example of regal justice, a bottomless spring of largess and benignity. He was in all the honest arts and faculties profoundly seen, in all liberal discipline equal with the best, in no kind of literature inexpert. He was to the world an ornament, to England a treasure, to his friends a comfort, to his foes a terrour, to his faithful and loving subjects a tender father, to innocents a sure protector, to wilful malefactors a sharp scourge, to his common weal and good people a quiet haven and anchor of safeguard, to the disturbers of the same a rock of extermination. In heinous and intolerable crimes against the commonwealth a severe judge, in like offences committed against himself a ready port and refuge of mercy, except to such as would persist incorrigibly. A man he was in gifts of nature and of grace peerless; and, to conclude, a man above all praises. Such a King did God set to reign over England; whereof this realm may well vaunt above other nations.

This is the portrait drawn without its shadows; yet the features described in the language of admiring exaggeration resemble the true image far more closely than the extravagant conception which floats in the modern belief. It is easy to understand how such a conception grew. Protestants and Catholics united to condemn a Government under which both had suffered, and a point on which enemies were agreed was assumed to be proved. When I commenced the examination of the records, I brought with me the inherited impression from which I had neither any thought nor any expectation that I should be disabused. I found that it melted between my hands, and with it disappeared that other fact so difficult to credit, yet as it had appeared so impossible to deny, that English parliaments, English judges, English clergy, statesmen whose beneficent legislature survives among the most valued of our institutions, prelates who were the founders and martyrs of the English Church, were the cowardly accomplices of abominable atrocities, and had disgraced themselves with a sycophancy which the Roman senate imperfectly approached when it fawned on Nero.

Henry had many faults. They have been exhibited in the progress of the narrative: I need not return to them. But his position was one of unexampled difficulty; and by the work which he accomplished, and the conditions, internal and external, under which his task was allotted to him, he, like every other man, ought to be judged. He was inconsistent; he can bear the reproach of it. He ended by accepting and approving what he had commenced with persecuting; yet it was with the honest inconsistency which distinguishes the conduct of most men of practical ability in times of change, and even by virtue of which they obtain their success. If at the commencement of the movement he had regarded the eucharist as a "remembrance," he must either have concealed his convictions or he would have forfeited his throne; if he had been a stationary bigot, the Reformation might have waited for a century, and would have been conquered only by an internecine war.

But as the nation moved the King moved, leading it, but not outrunning it; checking those who went too fast, dragging forward those who lagged behind. The conservatives, all that was sound and good among them, trusted him because he so long continued to share their conservatism; when he threw it aside he was not reproached with breach of confidence, because his own advance had accompanied theirs.

Protestants have exclaimed against the Six Articles Bill; Romanists against the Act of Supremacy. Philosophers complain that the prejudices of the people were needlessly violated, that opinions should have been allowed to be free, and the reform of religion have been left to be accomplished by reason. Yet, however cruel was the Six Articles Bill, the governing classes even among the laity were unanimous in its favour. The King was not converted by a sudden miracle; he believed the traditions in which he had been trained; his eyes, like the eyes of others, opened but slowly; and unquestionably, had he conquered for himself in their fulness the modern principles of toleration, he could not have governed by them a nation which was itself intolerant. Perhaps, of all living Englishmen who shared Henry's faith, there was not one so little desirous in himself of enforcing it by violence. His personal exertions were ever to mitigate the action of the law, while its letter was sustained; and England at its worst was a harbour of refuge to the Protestants compared to the Netherlands, to France, to Spain, or even to Scotland.

That the Romanists should have regarded him as a tyrant is natural; and were it true that English subjects owed fealty to the Pope, their feeling was just. But, however desirable it may be to leave religious opinion unfettered, it is certain that, if England was legitimately free, she could tolerate no difference of opinion on a question of allegiance, so long as Europe was conspiring to bring her back into slavery. So long as the English Romanists refused to admit without mental reservation that, if foreign enemies invaded this country in the Pope's name, their place must be at the side of their own sovereign, "religion" might palliate the moral guilt of their treason, but it could not exempt them from its punishment.

But these matters have been discussed in the details of this history, where alone they can be understood.

Beyond and besides the Reformation, the constitution of these islands now rests in large measure on foundations laid in this reign. Henry brought Ireland within the reach of English civilization. He absorbed Wales and the Palatinates into the general English system. He it was who raised the House of Commons from the narrow duty of voting supplies, and of passing without discussion the measures of the privy council, and converted them into the first power in the State under the Crown. When he ascended the throne so little did the Commons care for their privileges, that their attendance at the sessions of Parliament was enforced by a law. They woke into life in 1529, and they became the right hand of the King to subdue the resistance of the House of Lords, and to force upon them a course of legislation which from their hearts they detested. Other kings in times of difficulty summoned their "great councils," composed of peers, or prelates, or municipal officials, or any persons whom they pleased to nominate. Henry VIII broke through the ancient practice, and ever threw himself on the representatives of the people. By the Reformation, and by the power which he forced upon them, he had so interwoven the House of Commons with the highest business of the State, that the Peers thenceforward sunk to be their shadow.

Something, too, ought to be said of his individual exertions in the details of State administration. In his earlier life, though active and assiduous, he found leisure for elegant accomplishments, for splendid amusements, for relaxations careless, extravagant, sometimes questionable. As his life drew onwards his lighter tastes disappeared, and the whole energy of his intellect was pressed into the business of the commonwealth. Those who have examined the printed *State Papers* may form some impression of his industry from the documents which are his own composition, and the letters which he wrote and received: but only persons who have seen the original manuscripts, who have observed the traces of his pen in side notes and corrections, and the handwritings of his secretaries in diplomatic commissions, in drafts of Acts of Parliament, in expositions and formularies, in articles of faith, in proclamations, in the countless multitude of documents of all sorts, secular or ecclesiastical, which contain the real history of this extraordinary reign, only they can realize the extent of labour to which he sacrificed himself, and which brought his life to a premature close. His personal faults were great, and he shared, besides them, in the errors of his age; but far deeper blemishes would be but as scars upon the features of a sovereign who in trying times sustained nobly the honour of the English name, and carried the commonwealth securely through the hardest crisis in its history.

IF A LION KNEW HIS OWN STRENGTH

BISHOP WILLIAM STUBBS

Born in 1825, William Stubbs took an honors degree at Christ Church, Oxford, in 1848. By 1850 he was ordained priest (Anglican) and also was actively engaged in the study and editing of documents relevant to ecclesiastical and political history. His many activities included a Regius Professorship in Oxford, though that honor disappointed him in his hope of founding a thorough "historical school" there. After 1864 he increasingly devoted himself to private research, editing the texts of medieval authorities in the famed Rolls Series (19 volumes, 1864–89). But he is better known to English historians and educated laymen for his *Select Charters* and his three-volume *Constitutional History of England down to 1485,* which altered the study of medieval English history. Decidedly High Church, Stubbs was first Bishop of Chester and then of Oxford. After 1889 he all but abandoned historical work, devoting himself to episcopal administration until his death in 1901.

I SHALL NOT trouble you with any detailed reasons for my choice of a subject for this Term's statutory lectures; it is enough to observe that I have been busily employed upon the reign of Henry VIII for some months of ordinary lecturing, and that there is every probability that I may have to work upon him for some months to come. You will at once admit that Henry VIII is too big a subject to admit any rival on the same canvas, or under the same hand; whoever undertakes him at all must be content to devote himself for the time entirely to him.

* * *

From the very beginning of his reign, he is finding out what he can do; from the fall of Wolsey, and especially after the sacrifice of More, he is coming to regard what he can do as the only measure of what he ought to do: he is becoming the king for whom the kingdom is, the tyrant whose every caprice is wise and sacred: he turns the theory of kingship into action; the king can do no wrong; therefore men shall call right all that he does: he is the king, not an individual; what in an individual would be theft, is no theft in him; all property is the king's, he can take it, and he takes it; all that proceeds from his mouth is law; the king's heart is in the hand of the Lord, therefore all that comes out of the king's heart is the Lord's doing.[1]

Yet with all his grotesque and inhuman self-absorption, the miserable and growing result of the long tenure of irresponsible power, we cannot wisely deny the king some great qualities besides mere force. Contemporary foreigners, the justice of whose general judgment is amply proved by later history, and whose opinion, according to Lord Bacon's dictum, is generally that which future ages will be found to confirm, are unanimous in their glorification of Henry's personal and mental gifts. His beauty was of that sort that commended

[1] Stubbs is here commenting on two maxims of civil law: "Whatever pleases the Prince has the force of Law," and "The King is given for the Kingdom, not the Kingdom for the King" — or rather the negations of such principles.

From William Stubbs, *Seventeen Lectures on the Study of Medieval and Modern History and Kindred Subjects* (Oxford, 1900), pp. 241, 246–47, 253–55 and 257–62. Reprinted by permission of The Clarendon Press, Oxford.

itself to the taste of those times. And more than that: for the painters of his portrait have succeeded in giving him an individuality and a humanity which shows either that he possessed a remarkable physique, or that they took more pains with him than they did with his wives — the deadly-lively sort of ladies whose portraits are, if not a justification, at least a colourable occasion for understanding the readiness with which he put them away. Henry's portrait, I said, would fill any canvas; and, allowing for what must be allowed for, dress, expression, and attitude, it must be allowed to be the portrait of a personable king.

His mental abilities I rank very high: he had been carefully educated by good scholars, and had made remarkable progress; not so great, Lord Bacon tells us, as his brother Arthur; but still remarkable at a remarkable time: he did not let his knowledge acquired in boyhood fade out of his mind: after his accession he must have continued his reading; his book against Luther, which, whatever assistance he may have received, was in conception and execution entirely his own, was an extraordinary work for a young king;[2] and the intelligent interest which, down to the last, he showed in religious and other ecclesiastical questions, even when he was most capricious and peremptory, evinces both memory and a real appreciation of subjects on which contemporary kings thought it sinful to think at all. If it were not for the miserable self-will and self-worship which runs through these, there might be something to admire.

Well, it is not for us to judge. The king is apart from other men in his opportunities, in his excuses, in his temptations; even in his responsibility for the direct results of his acts; and he must stand alone in the judgment. But I will leave the remaining sentiments or reflexions which suggest themselves, to be justified after the review of the reign which I propose to take now.

[2] The famous *Defense of the Seven Sacraments* of 1521.

*   *   *

It is clear, from the beginning of his reign, that Henry was a prince who had only to learn the extent of his powers, in order to attempt to exercise them. If we may believe the law reporters, as early as 1515 he had declared himself determined not to allow any superiority of external spiritual courts in a country of which he was sovereign; and there are signs, in Wolsey's history, that the imminent danger of the king's taking advantage of the Statute of Praemunire[3] was in his mind long before he was actually sacrificed. But the earlier years of the reign were remarkably free from occasions on which any great constitutional crisis could arise. Henry's ambition, like Wolsey's, was mainly set upon an influential place in the councils of Europe, and among the people at large there was contentment. Henry had been brought up very strictly, and married, very young, to a wife to whom he gave his full affection; the good impressions of his training were, at least for several years, strong enough to keep him out of the domestic scandals that divide courts; and although Bessie Blount and the Duke of Richmond[4] became prominent about ten years after the reign begins, it is not until 1524 or 1525 that the divorce question even looms in the distance. Up to that time the want of constitutional principle in the king and his minister has been chiefly apparent in the matter of money-getting. Soon after this Henry seems to have fallen in love with Anne Boleyn, and to have begun to contemplate the divorce. The mere formalities of obtaining such a divorce were not formidable; but the parties interested in preventing it were very formidable indeed. The emperor was the

[3] A group of statutes passed between 1352 and 1393. They were designed to protect the King's rights against interference by foreign courts, i.e., against the papal court's meddling with rights of ecclesiastical property. By the sixteenth century their meaning was expanded to protect the secular courts of the realm against the spiritual courts, even though after 1534 courts ecclesiastical were also courts under the Crown.

[4] Henry Fitzroy (1519–1536), Henry VIII's natural son by Elizabeth Blount.

queen's nephew. The pope's power was being rudely shaken both in Germany and in Italy. To be brief; the pope was prevailed on to commission Wolsey and Campegio to determine the validity of the king's marriage; when the trial had begun, the cause was called back to Rome; Henry felt that his only chance of getting the divorce was to have it tried in England; the pope felt that the only chance of avoiding a crisis, in which between Henry and Charles he must certainly either temporally or spiritually be ruined, was to keep the discussion languidly dragging on at Rome until the parties were tired, or something else turned up. This, thus early, Henry had the sense to see; he therefore destroyed Wolsey, and that by the very Statute of Praemunire at the evasion of which he had so long connived: his eyes were opened to the powers of the Praemunire, and in his confiscation of Wolsey's estates he had his first taste of spoil. He saw that the Praemunire made him absolutely master of the clergy, and, as absolute master, the primary owner of all Church property. Hence the great chain of ecclesiastical statutes follows in an order that we might almost dignify by the name of Evolution.[5] As lord and master of the Church, he could utilise Church machinery to obtain the divorce and the marriage on which he had set his king's heart; and, when he was tired of the second wife, he could obtain, from the archbishop he had made, an annulling of that marriage as easily as he could obtain a Bill of Attainder from the parliament; and, when in time he married another woman whom he did not like, he could by a commission to the national synod obtain another judgment of nullity of marriage, and by negotiating with parliament another petition for another marriage. This wonderful Praemunire, of which the foreign residents at the English court speaks with horror as a mystery of which the king alone possessed the key, might be a lash brandished over laity and clergy alike so long as the papal supremacy was admitted by either.

Thus the desire of spoil, the ambition of uncontrolled sovereignty, and the facilities of gaining his own immediate ends in marriage, urged on the king in the line of doing, not what he ought, but what he could.

* * *

But, having gone so far, why not go a little further? In the parliament of 1533 he obtained the passing of the Statute of Appeals, founded on what seems to be the true theory of Church and State; forbidding the carrying of appeals to Rome at all, and providing sufficient machinery for appeals at home: the Annates Bill[6] had provided for the confirmation and consecration of bishops, and the two together proclaimed with one breath the emancipation of the Church from Roman supremacy, and its competence for complete internal administration under the supremacy of the king. But from this moment the ecclesiastical reforms became involved more and more with the king's marriage policy. Anne Boleyn, her father, and Cranmer, who seems to have been their family counsellor, were bent on further measures of hostility to Rome; and Cromwell, who was the king's minister rather than the queen's, was likewise politically a protestant. The year 1534 saw the clergy, both secular and regular, compelled to make a new submission, to recognise the validity of the marriage and the succession, and to admit a new and comprehensive oath for the maintenance of the two. A new statute of appeals, founded on the Submission of 1532, modified the appellate jurisdiction, and furnished a recourse to the king in chancery as the final reference which in the former statute had been left to the Archbishop and, in causes touching the king, to the Upper House of Convocation; a new statute on Annates reformed the regulations

[5] Stubbs' emphasis on "evolution" is characteristic of those who see in the English Reformation the unfolding of a plan already in Henry VIII's mind in 1529. Contrast this view with that of G. R. Elton given below.

[6] It also turned certain profits of church livings from Roman into royal coffers.

for the appointment of bishops; the synodical declaration which denied the authority of Rome, and a statute which forbade all payments to Rome, swept away all signs of the old subjection.

But there is no step, in parliament at least, towards doctrinal change: the law of heresy is reformed but not made less stringent, and it is no longer heretical to speak against the pope. Even in the Articles of 1536 the progress towards change is defined by the simple elimination of distinctive papal doctrine;[7] the convocation urges an authorised translation of Holy Scripture as the best antidote to heresy. But events were proceeding more rapidly than ideas: the oath of succession necessitated the imprisonment of More and Fisher; a second session in the autumn of 1534 gave the secular recognition to the king's style as supreme head on earth of the Church of England; that title was publicly promulgated by letters patent in January, 1535; and the accusation of attempting to deprive the king of this designation brought the two worthiest men in England to the block during the summer of that year. The death of Fisher, the confidential friend of his father and grandmother, and that of More, who represented all that was good in his own early experience, whether they were wrung from him by the importunities of his wife, or coldly acquiesced in as cases in which all human feeling must be sunk before the self-idolatry of the theoretic kingship, seem to prove and to have proved to the king himself that no scruples should ever hereafter touch him.

The next step of change was the dissolution of the smaller monasteries: Wolsey, in his great scheme for church reforms, had led the way to this. He had seen the increasing importance of the great towns of England, and the increasing mischief caused by the incurable uselessness of the monastic foundations; and he had obtained bulls of legation from Rome enabling him to suppress convents and establish bishoprics. That had opened the king's eyes to a new possibility, and, although he waited several years before he executed his scheme, all that was good in the scheme was Wolsey's, all that was bad in it wears an unfortunate air of having been done by Cromwell. But it was almost a point of honour with Henry to show that without the pope he could do all that Wolsey had been empowered to do. So in the autumn of 1535 Cromwell and his agents effected a visitation of the monasteries, the report of which insured their condemnation;[8] and, in the last session of the Long Parliament in 1536, the dissolution of the smaller houses was decreed. A new court, the Court of Augmentations,[9] was founded to manage the property which by the same act was vested in the king and his heirs. The greater monasteries survived a little longer, and in their case the process of surrender took the place of a general and compulsory dissolution. In the session of 1539, however, a similar act vested in the king the property of the surrendered houses, and in that year the abbots disappeared from parliament. At the same time the king was empowered to establish new bishoprics; suffragan bishops had been the subject of legislation in 1534, when the act was passed which supplied to the more aged and busy prelates the assistance that had been hitherto furnished by titular bishops in partibus commissioned at Rome.

These acts very nearly complete the series by which Henry evolved the idea of a regal papacy out of the royal supremacy. For some subordinate purposes, as for dispensations and faculties, he allowed the Archbishop of Canterbury to exercise a quasi-legatine authority under himself, and with a check in Chancery on his proceedings; but in all such matters he was himself the fountain of power. The climax was reached when, by the appointment of Cromwell as Vicar-General, with an author-

---

[7] The "Ten Articles" were replaced in 1539 by the more orthodox "Six Articles."

[8] These reports, or comperta, are thoroughly discussed in Dom David Knowles' book and in G. Baskerville (see the Suggestions for Additional Reading).

[9] Financial business was done in curial and juridical forms: thus, the Court of the Exchequer, etc.

ity and precedence above all prelates and nobles, he emulated the papal assumption of exercising direct powers through a legate *a latere*. Unluckily for himself and for Henry also, the royal legate *a latere* proved too great a power to manage; meddled with too many things, provoked too much hostility, got his feet entangled in the marriage net he had provided for the old lion, and perished more sadly, because more ignominiously, than his predecessors in power and ruin.

I have spoken thus far mainly of Henry's ecclesiastical measures as they affected endowments and jurisdictions; but there is a side, the side of doctrine, which is not less important. He never forgot that he was the defender of the faith; nor, whatever were his eccentricities and aberrations in minor particulars, does he seem ever to have gone in this region further in the direction of change than the more enlightened popes and cardinals of his own age would have gone. Wolsey would have agreed with him in the dissolution of the monasteries; the convocation had petitioned for a translation of the Bible; the worship of the saints and the excessive devotions at their shrines had long been a burden to the souls of men, not merely men like Erasmus, but of far more unimpeachable orthodoxy. The supremacy of the chair of S. Peter was by no means as yet an article of unquestioning faith; even the marriage of the clergy was a point not beyond discussion. But there were things which, quite irrespective of the pope and his claims, could not be touched without the taint of heresy. And of these Henry, with all his inconsistencies, was a constant defender. He might tolerate a certain evangelical obliquity in Boleyn's eyes; he might choose to be blind to Cromwell's sympathies with foreign protestantism; he might tolerate Mrs. Cranmer,[10] as he had not looked too curiously into the semi-matrimonial connexions of the great cardinal; he might even go to the length

of marrying a lady like Anne of Cleves, in whom, through the phlegmatic impenetrability of the Flanders mare, some instincts of unorthodox skittishness might be detected. But Henry was royally orthodox. If, for any purpose of the moment, he relaxed the stringency of the courts, he kept the law very strong against heresy. This acted in a curious way. The king's idea that he was supreme in Church and State, whilst in some regions it led him to maintain the administrative machinery of the two severely separate, in others led him to some mixture of his functions. In his first act of heresy he repealed the statute of Henry IV "de hereticis comburendis"[11] which seemed to give too much power to the bishops, but re-enacted those of Richard II and Henry V which tended to make heresy an offence at common law. A similar intention is clear in the Act of Six Articles of 1539, and with this light upon it, in the several modifications of the Six Articles which were proposed in the later parliaments. I shall not speculate on the possibility that, if he had lived longer, he might have developed more in the direction of protestant doctrine; I think however that it is unlikely; doctrinally, although quite able to maintain his own line, he clearly symbolised consistently with Gardiner and not with Cranmer. The extinction of the Norfolk interest might have led him to further negotiations with protestantism abroad, but with domestic puritanism, such as that by which Somerset[12] palliated his greed for confiscation, there is no trace in Henry. For spoil however the old lion went on yearning to the last; the dissolution of chantries and colleges, to follow that of the monasteries, was one of the measures of his last parliament.

It may strike some of us that the process

---

[10] Cranmer had married contrary to canon law while on embassy in Germany, *before* his appointment to Canterbury.

[11] "For the burning of heretics," passed in the anti-Lollard commotions of the early fifteenth century.

[12] Sir Edward Seymore, Duke of Somerset, Protector at the beginning of Edward VI's reign. Stubbs' use of the word "Puritan" must be taken with a grain of salt. It has recently been argued that Seymore's views were Erasmian.

of change had now gone far enough; the English Church was freed from the yoke of Rome, but she retained all her proper framework and at least half of her old endowments; I say at least half, I should not like to commit myself to a statement that there was much more. She had obtained the Bible in English and the use of the chief forms of prayer in the vernacular, and was preparing for a revision in form of the Sacramental Services; she had rid herself of a mass of superstitious usages. It is true that the king remained a believer in Roman Catholic forms of doctrine; but it must always be remembered that those forms had not yet, by the Tridentine decrees,[13] been hardened into their later inflexibility; and, when we consider the terrible risks which, in the next reign, the Church of England ran, of losing all sense or desire of continuity, identity, or communion with the historic Catholic Christendom, we may feel thankful that such risk was run under a weak king and feeble ministers, not under the influence of a strong will and strong hand like Henry's.

You will see thus that I believe him to have been a man of purpose; not the mere capricious tyrant who found it a pleasant exercise of despotic power to burn Catholics and Protestants on the same day, or found a malicious gratification in making Cranmer support the Catholic doctrine of the Eucharist and Gardiner the doctrine of unlimited obedience: further than this I do not go. I believe him to have been a man of unbounded selfishness; a man to whom the acquisition of power was pre-cious mainly as a step towards the acquisition of greater power; a man of whom we may say, as I said at first, that he was the king, the whole king, and nothing but the king; that he wished to be, with regard to the Church of England, the pope, the whole pope, and something more than pope. You remember how in his early days Maximilian had tempted him with the offer of the Empire, he himself to retire on the popedom with an inchoate claim to canonization. Henry was determined to have in England at least both Empire and Papacy, to make the best, or rather the most, of both worlds.

I have said more than in proper proportion I ought to have said with reference to Henry's ecclesiastical policy, and left but little time for the analogous features that may be traced in his temporal policy: one reason for that is the greater interest we all feel in the religious question of the Reformation; another is in the fact that his ecclesiastical measures had a much more lasting consequence than his temporal ones. We have long rid ourselves of all the secular burdens imposed by what we call the Tudor dictatorship, but we are still living under religious or ecclesiastical conditions that owe very much, even of their present form, to the hand of Henry. You will, I hope, know me too well to misinterpret me in these expressions; you will not suspect me of making Henry VIII the founder of the Church of England; but I do not conceal from myself that, under the Divine power which brings good out of evil and over-rules the wrath of man to the praise of God, we have received good as well as evil through the means of this "majestic lord who broke the bonds of Rome."

[13] The decrees of the Council of Trent (1542–1563).

THE TYRANNY OF TUDOR TIMES

ALFRED F. POLLARD

Alfred F. Pollard was born in 1869. After a distinguished undergraduate career at Jesus College, Oxford, he took an M.A. in history. He was the author of many studies of the Tudor period, among them his classic *Wolsey* and biographies of Cranmer and Protector Somerset. He was also the recipient of many honors and prizes, the chief of which were the Lothian Prize and the Arnold Prize. He was a fellow of both the British Academy and the Royal Historical Society. But perhaps his greatest contribution to historical studies was his founding of the Institute of Historical Research, London, and the *Bulletin* of that Institute.

So DIED and so was buried the most remarkable man who ever sat on the English throne. His reign, like his character, seems to be divided into two inconsistent halves. In 1519 his rule is pronounced more suave and gentle than the greatest liberty anywhere else; twenty years later terror is said to reign supreme. It is tempting to sum up his life in one sweeping generalisation, and to say that it exhibits a continuous development of Henry's intellect and deterioration of his character. Yet it is difficult to read the King's speech in Parliament at the close of 1545 without crediting him with some sort of ethical ideas and aims; his life was at least as free from vice during the last, as during the first, seven years of his reign; in seriousness of purpose and steadfastness of aim it was immeasurably superior; and at no time did Henry's moral standard vary greatly from that of many whom the world is content to regard as its heroes. His besetting sin was egotism, a sin which princes can hardly, and Tudors could nowise, avoid. Of egotism Henry had his full share from the beginning; at first it moved in a limited, personal sphere, but gradually it extended its scope till it comprised the whole realm of national religion and policy. The obsta-

cles which he encountered in prosecuting his suit for a divorce from Catherine of Aragon were the first check he experienced in the gratification of a personal whim, and the effort to remove those impediments drew him on to the world-wide stage of the conflict with Rome. He was ever proceeding from the particular to the general, from an attack on a special dispensation to an attack on the dispensing power of the Pope, and thence to an assault on the whole edifice of papal claims. He started with no desire to separate England from Rome, or to reform the Anglican Church; those aims he adopted, little by little, as subsidiary to the attainment of his one great personal purpose. He arrived at his principles by a process of deduction from his own particular case.

As Henry went on, his "quick and penetrable eyes," as More described them, were more and more opened to the extent of what he could do; and he realised, as he said, how small was the power of the Pope. Papal authority had always depended on moral influence and not on material resources. That moral influence had long been impaired; the sack of Rome in 1527 afforded further demonstration of its impotence; and when Clement condoned that

From Alfred F. Pollard, *Henry VIII* (London, 1902), pp. 343–53. Reprinted by permission of Longmans, Green and Co. Ltd.

outrage, and formed a close alliance with the chief offender, the Papacy suffered a blow from which it never recovered. Temporal princes might continue to recognise the Pope's authority, but it was only because they chose, and not because they were compelled so to do; they supported him, not as the divinely commissioned Vicar of Christ, but as a useful instrument in the prosecution of their own and their people's desires. It is called a theological age, but it was also irreligious, and its principal feature was secularisation. National interests had already become the dominant factor in European politics; they were no longer to be made subservient to the behests of the universal Church. The change was tacitly or explicitly recognised everywhere; and *cujus regio, ejus religio* was the principle upon which German ecclesiastical politics were based at the Peace of Augsburg.[1] It was assumed that each prince could do what he liked in his own country; they might combine to make war on an excommunicate king, but only if war suited their secular policy; and the rivalry between Francis and Charles was so keen that each set greater store upon Henry's help than upon his destruction.

Thus the breach with Rome was made a possible, though not an easy, task; and Henry was left to settle the matter at home with little to fear from abroad, except threats which he knew to be empty. England was the key to the situation, and in England must be sought the chief causes of Henry's success. If we are to believe that Henry's policy was at variance with the national will, his reign must remain a political mystery, and we can offer no explanation of the facts that Henry was permitted to do his work at all, and that it has stood so long the test of time. He had, no doubt, exceptional facilities for getting his way. His dictatorship was the child of the Wars of the Roses, and his people, conscious of the fact that Henry was their only

bulwark against the recurrence of civil strife, and bound up as they were in commercial and industrial pursuits, were willing to bear with a much more arbitrary government than they would have been in less perilous times. The alternatives may have been evil, but the choice was freely made. No government, whatever its form, whatever its resources, can permanently resist the national will; every nation has, roughly speaking, the government it deserves and desires, and a popular vote would never in Henry's reign have decreed his deposition. The popular mind may be ill-informed, distorted by passion and prejudice, and formed on selfish motives. Temporarily, too, the popular will may be neutralised by skilful management on the part of the government, by dividing its enemies and counterworking their plans; and of all those arts Henry was a past master. But such expedients cannot prevail in the end; in 1553 the Duke of Northumberland[2] had a subtle intellect and all the machinery of Tudor government at his disposal; Queen Mary had not a man, nor a shilling. Yet Mary, by popular favour, prevailed without shedding a drop of blood. Henry himself was often compelled to yield to his people. Abject self-abasement on their part and stupendous power of will on Henry's, together provide no adequate solution for the history of his reign.

With all his self-will, Henry was never blind to the distinction between what he could and what he could not do. Strictly speaking, he was a constitutional king; he neither attempted to break up Parliament, nor to evade the law. He combined in his royal person the parts of despot and demagogue, and both he clothed in Tudor grace and majesty. He led his people in the way they wanted to go, he tempted them with the baits they coveted most, he humoured their prejudices against the clergy and against the pretensions of Rome, and he

[1] The principle that the religion of a territory should follow that of the ruler: "whose territory, his religion."

[2] Sir John Dudley, son of the early Tudor official Edmund Dudley, who was executed in 1510, and the father of the great Elizabethan Earl of Leicester, Robert Dudley.

used every concession to extract some fresh material for building up his own authority. He owed his strength to the skill with which he appealed to the weaknesses of a people whose prevailing characteristics were a passion for material prosperity and an absolute indifference to human suffering. "We," wrote one of Henry's Secretaries of State, "we, which talk much of Christ and His Holy Word, have, I fear me, used a much contrary way; for we leave fishing of men, and fish again in the tempestuous seas of this world for gain and wicked Mammon." A few noble examples, Catholic and Protestant, redeemed, by their blood, the age from complete condemnation, but, in the mass of his subjects, the finer feelings seem to have been lost in the pursuit of wealth. There is no sign that the hideous tortures inflicted on men condemned for treason, or the equally horrible sufferings of heretics burnt at the stake, excited the least qualm of compassion in the breast of the multitude; the Act of Six Articles seems to have been rather a popular measure, and the multiplication of treasons evoked no national protest.

Henry, indeed, was the typical embodiment of an age that was at once callous and full of national vigour, and his failings were as much a source of strength as his virtues. His defiance of the conscience of Europe did him no harm in England, where the splendid isolation of *Athanasius contra mundum* is always a popular attitude;[3] and even his bitterest foes could scarce forbear to admire the dauntless front he presented to every peril. National pride was the highest motive to which he appealed. For the rest, he based his power on his people's material interests, and not on their moral instincts. He took no such hold of the ethical nature of men as did Oliver Cromwell, but he was liked none the less for that; for the nation regarded Cromwell, the man of God, with much less

favour than Charles II, the man of sin; and statesmen who try to rule on exclusively moral principles are seldom successful and seldom beloved. Henry's successor, Protector Somerset, made a fine effort to introduce some elements of humanity into the spirit of government; but he perished on the scaffold, while his colleagues denounced his gentleness and love of liberty, and declared that his repeal of Henry's savage treason-laws was the worst deed done in their generation.

The King avoided the error of the Protector; he was neither behind nor before the average man of the time; he appealed to the mob, and the mob applauded. *Salus populi*, he said in effect, *suprema lex*, and the people agreed;[4] for that is a principle which suits demagogues no less than despots, though they rarely possess Henry's skill in working it out. Henry, it is true, modified the maxim slightly by substituting prince for people, and by practising, before it was preached, Louis XIV's doctrine that *L'État, c'est moi*.[5] But the assumption that the welfare of the people was bound up with that of their King was no idle pretence; it was based on solid facts, the force of which the people themselves admitted. They endorsed the tyrant's plea of necessity. The pressure of foreign rivalries, and the fear of domestic disruption, convinced Englishmen of the need for despotic rule, and no consideration whatever was allowed to interfere with the stability of government; individual rights and even the laws themselves must be overridden, if they conflicted with the interests of the State. Torture was illegal in England, and men were proud of the fact, yet, in cases of treason, when the national security was thought to be involved, torture was freely used, and it was used by the very men who boasted of England's immunity. They were conscious of no inconsistency; the common law was very well as a general rule, but

---

[3] "Athanasius against the World." The reference is to the Bishop of Alexandria who, in the fourth century A.D., opposed the dominant Arian heretics in Egypt.

[4] "The well-being of the people is the highest law."

[5] "I am the State."

the highest law of all was the welfare of the State.

This was the real tyranny of Tudor times; men were dominated by the idea that the State was the be-all and end-all of human existence. In its early days the State is a child; it has no will and no ideas of its own, and its first utterances are merely imitation and repetition. But by Henry VIII's reign the State in England had grown to lusty manhood; it dismissed its governess, the Church, and laid claim to that omnipotence and absolute sovereignty which Hobbes regretfully expounded in his *Leviathan.* The idea supplied an excuse to despots and an inspiration to noble minds. "Surely," wrote a genuine patriot in 1548, "every honest man ought to refuse no pains, no travail, no study, he ought to care for no reports, no slanders, no displeasure, no envy, no malice, so that he might profit the commonwealth of his country, for whom next after God he is created." The service of the State tended, indeed, to encroach on the service of God, and to obliterate altogether respect for individual liberty. Wolsey on his deathbed was visited by qualms of conscience, but, as a rule, victims to the principle afford, by their dying words, the most striking illustrations of the omnipotence of the idea. Condemned traitors are concerned on the scaffold, not to assert their innocence, but to proclaim their readiness to die as an example of obedience to the law. However unfair the judicial methods of Tudor times may seem to us, the sufferers always thank the King for granting them free trial. Their guilt or innocence is a matter of little moment; the one thing needful is that no doubt should be thrown on the inviolability of the will of the State; and the audience commend them. They are not expected to confess or to express contrition, but merely to submit to the decrees of the nation; if they do that, they are said to make a charitable and godly end, and they deserve the respect and sympathy of men; if not, they die uncharitably, and are held up to reprobation. To an age like that there was nothing strange in the

union of State and Church and the supremacy of the King over both; men professed Christianity in various forms, but to all men alike the State was their real religion, and the King was their great High Priest. The sixteenth century, and especially the reign of Henry VIII, supplies the most vivid illustration of the working, both for good and for evil, of the theory that the individual should be subordinate in goods, in life and in conscience to the supreme dictates of the national will. This theory was put into practice by Henry VIII long before it was made the basis of any political philosophy, just as he practised Erastianism before Erastus gave it a name.[6]

The devotion paid to the State in Tudor times inevitably made expediency, and not justice or morality, the supreme test of public acts. The dictates of expediency were, indeed, clothed in legal forms, but laws are primarily intended to secure neither justice nor morality, but the interests of the State; and the highest penalty known to the law is inflicted for high treason, a legal and political crime which does not necessarily involve any breach whatever of the code of morals. Traitors are not executed because they are immoral, but because they are dangerous. Never did a more innocent head fall on the scaffold than that of Lady Jane Grey;[7] never was an execution more fully justified by the law. The contrast was almost as flagrant in many a State trial in the reign of Henry VIII; no king was so careful of law, but he was not so careful of justice. Therein lay his safety, for the law takes no cognisance of injustice, unless the injustice is also a breach of the law, and Henry rarely, if ever, broke the law. Not only did he keep

[6] Erastus, or Liebler of Heidelberg, a physician who opposed the Calvinist doctrine of excommunication in the sixteenth century. His name is given to the doctrine of state supremacy in ecclesiastic matters by an erroneous convention.

[7] Daughter of Henry Grey, Duke of Suffolk; Lady Jane was a humanist prodigy married to Guilford Dudley as part of Northumberland's plot to alter the Tudor succession in 1553. She was executed for her part in the conspiracy, though she was not yet seventeen.

the law, but he contrived that the nation should always proclaim the legality of his conduct. Acts of attainder, his favourite weapon, are erroneously supposed to have been the method to which he resorted for removing opponents whose conviction he could not obtain by a legal trial. But acts of attainder were, as a rule, supplements to, not substitutes for, trials by jury; many were passed against the dead, whose goods had already been forfeited to the King as the result of judicial verdicts. Moreover, convictions were always easier to obtain from juries than acts of attainder from Parliament. It was simplicity itself to pack a jury of twelve, and even a jury of peers; but it was a much more serious matter to pack both Houses of Parliament. What then was the meaning and use of acts of attainder? They were acts of indemnity for the King. People might cavil at the verdict of juries; for they were only the decisions of a handful of men; but who should impugn the voice of the whole body politic expressed in its most solemn, complete and legal form? There is no way, said Francis to Henry in 1532, so safe as by Parliament, and one of Henry's invariable methods was to make the whole nation, so far as he could, his accomplice. For pardons and acts of grace the King was ready to assume the responsibility; but the nation itself must answer for rigorous deeds. And acts of attainder were neither more nor less than deliberate pronouncements, on the part of the people, that it was expedient that one man should die rather than that the whole nation should perish or run any risk of danger.

History, in a democratic age, tends to become a series of popular apologies, and is inclined to assume that the people can do no wrong; some one must be the scapegoat for the people's sins, and the national sins of Henry's reign are all laid on Henry's shoulders. But the nation in the sixteenth century deliberately condoned injustice, when injustice made for its peace. It has done so before and after, and may possibly do so again. It is easy in England to-day to denounce the cruel sacrifices imposed on individuals in the time of Henry VIII by their subordination in everything to the interests of the State but, whenever and wherever like dangers have threatened, recourse has been had to similar methods, to government by proclamation, to martial law, and to verdicts based on political expediency.

The contrast between morals and politics, which comes out in Henry's reign as a terrible contradiction, is inherent in all forms of human society. Politics, the action of men in the mass, are akin to the operation of natural forces; and, as such, they are neither moral nor immoral; they are simply non-moral. Political movements are often as resistless as the tides of the ocean; they carry to fortune, and they bear to ruin, the just and the unjust with heedless impartiality. Cato and Brutus striving against the torrent of Roman imperialism, Fisher and More seeking to stem the secularisation of the Church, are like those who would save men's lives from the avalanche by preaching to the mountain on the text of the sixth commandment. The efforts of good men to avert a sure but cruel fate are the truest theme of the Tragic Muse; and it is possible to represent Henry's reign as one long nightmare of "truth for ever on the scaffold, wrong for ever on the throne"; for Henry VIII embodied an inevitable movement of politics, while Fisher and More stood only for individual conscience.

That is the secret of Henry's success. He directed the storm of a revolution which was doomed to come, which was certain to break those who refused to bend, and which may be explained by natural causes, but cannot be judged by moral considerations. The storm cleared the air and dissipated many a pestilent vapour, but it left a trail of wreck and ruin over the land. The nation purchased political salvation at the price of moral debasement; the individual was sacrificed on the altar of the State; and popular subservience proved the impossibility of saving a people from itself. Constitutional guarantees are worthless without the national will to maintain them; men lightly abandon what they lightly hold; and in Henry's reign, the English spirit of independence burned low in its socket, and love of freedom grew cold. The indifference of his subjects to political issues tempted Henry along the path to tyranny, and despotic power developed in him features, the repulsiveness of which cannot be concealed by the most exquisite art, appealing to the most deep-rooted prejudice. He turned to his own profit the needs and the faults of his people, as well as their national spirit. He sought the greatness of England, and he spared no toil in the quest; but his labours were spent for no ethical purpose. His aims were selfish; his realm must be strong, because he must be great. He had the strength of a lion, and like a lion he used it.

Yet it is probable that Henry's personal influence and personal action averted greater evils than those they provoked. Without him, the storm of the Reformation would still have burst over England; without him, it might have been far more terrible. Every drop of blood shed under Henry VIII might have been a river under a feebler king. Instead of a stray execution here and there, conducted always with a scrupulous regard for legal forms, wars of religion might have desolated the land and swept away thousands of lives. London saw many a hideous sight in Henry's reign, but it had no cause to envy the Catholic capitals which witnessed the sack of Rome and the massacre of St. Bartholomew; for all Henry's iniquities, multiplied manifold, would not equal the volume of murder and sacrilege wrought at Rome in May, 1527, or at Paris in August, 1572. From such

orgies of violence and crime England was saved by the strong right arm and the iron will of her Tudor king. "He is," said Wolsey after his fall, "a prince of royal courage, and he hath a princely heart; and rather than he will miss or want part of his appetite he will hazard the loss of one-half of his kingdom." But Henry discerned more clearly than Wolsey the nature of the ground on which he stood; by accident, or by design, his appetite conformed to potent and permanent forces; and wherein it did not, he was, in spite of Wolsey's remark, content to forgo its gratification. It was not he, but the Reformation, which put the kingdoms of Europe to the hazard. The Sphinx propounded her riddle to all nations alike, and all were required to answer. Should they cleave to the old, or should they embrace the new? Some pressed forward, others held back, and some, to their own confusion, replied in dubious tones. Surrounded by faint hearts and fearful minds, Henry VIII neither faltered nor failed. He ruled in a ruthless age with a ruthless hand, he dealt with a violent crisis by methods of blood and iron, and his measures were crowned with whatever sanction worldly success can give. He is Machiavelli's *Prince* in action. He took his stand on efficiency rather than principle, and symbolised the prevailing of the gates of Hell. The spiritual welfare of England entered into his thoughts, if at all, as a minor consideration; but for her peace and material comfort it was well that she had as her King, in her hour of need, a man, and a man who counted the cost, who faced the risk, and who did with his might whatsoever his hand found to do.

THE ENGLISH SCHISM:
OCCASION AND CAUSE

GUSTAVE CONSTANT

Gustave Constant was born in 1869 in the Vendée and after close studies in literature and diplomatics at l'Ecole des Hautes-Etudes he spent three years in the French College at Rome. In 1893 he was ordained a Roman Catholic priest. For some years he pursued archival research abroad, until in 1908 he was named Professor of Modern Church History at the Catholic Institute in Paris. Gravely wounded while on active service in the Dardanelles campaign of the First World War, Constant refused to slacken the pace of his studies or teaching and traveled widely in Europe, Africa, and the United States after 1918. Before his death in 1940 he published many important books and articles, many of them about sixteenth-century church history. Among his chief works are: *La Réforme en Angleterre*, 2 volumes; *La Légation du Cardinal Morone près de l'empereur et le concile de Trente* and his *Concession à l'Allemagne de la communion sous les deux espèces*, 2 volumes.

THE OCCASION of the English Schism is so patent and indisputable that many people scarcely trouble to look for the causes, while some even think that the occasion of it, Henry VIII's divorce, was in reality the cause. That is certainly a short, easy and simple solution, but truth is — generally — more complicated than that. In his *English Law and The Renaissance* Maitland[1] admits that the history of the Reformation in England is complicated. To attribute everything to the king's despotism and the people's servility is an easy way of dealing with the subject, but it has the disadvantage of mistaking the effect for the cause. For it was precisely in his conflict with Rome that Henry's eyes were opened and he saw how far his power might be extended. "If the lion knew his own strength, hard were it for any man to rule him," said Thomas More to Cromwell, al-

luding to the king. But the lion was not yet aware that its claws had grown; and it experimented with them on the Church. We must then discover what it was that allowed the king to meddle with the Church and the Reformation to spring up and develop on English soil.

Henry VIII's Schism was but an episode in the eternal conflict between Church and State, and in England this conflict was not new. Who has not heard of the terrible struggles between Alexander III and Henry II in the twelfth, and between Innocent III and John Lackland in the thirteenth century, struggles which ended in humiliation for the royal power? It would almost seem that the memory of that humiliation had not been forgotten. "For his part, Henry VIII meant to remedy it," wrote the imperial ambassador in 1533, "and repair the error of Kings Henry II and John, who, by deceit, being in difficulties, had made this realm and Ireland tributary."

A few days before his death Warham,

[1] F. W. Maitland was perhaps the greatest English legal scholar and historian of his time; he died in 1906.

From Gustave Constant, *The Reformation in England* (London, 1940), pp. 1–8 and 21–34. Reprinted by permission of Sheed and Ward Ltd., London, and of Harper and Row, Publishers, New York.

the Archbishop of Canterbury, said that the king was beginning to follow in the path of Henry II and that his policy resembled the Clarendon Constitutions (1164).[2] Had he not already shown, in 1515, his aversion to the Church's liberties and his desire to make the Church his servant? "We are King of England; and the King of England in times past never had any superior but God. . . . You interpret your decrees at your pleasure; but, as for me, I will never consent to your desire any more than my progenitors have done." From William the Conqueror to the death of Edward III, for three centuries the Crown and Parliament elaborated a long series of decrees and statutes tending to restrain papal jurisdiction in England; these were a source of inspiration at the time of the Schism.[3]

Henry VIII succeeded where Henry II failed because the sixteenth century was no longer the twelfth. The medieval ideal of unity, bringing the various parts of Christendom together in one body under a single temporal head and a single spiritual head, had been succeeded by a national spirit, which is essentially separatist and has for effect division and partition. The spiritual unity was immediately weakened. Northern Europe broke up into independent national churches, which were proud of having shaken off what they termed the papal yoke. When the Church in England broke with Rome and the king made himself its supreme head very few voices were raised in protest.

Papal authority had suffered a gradual eclipse which deepened more and more during the captivity at Avignon and during the Great Schism in the West, a period of moral confusion and corruption. Richard II (1377–1399) and Henry IV (1399–1413) took advantage of this to deprive the papacy of a part of its temporal rights, and

the primate of England (1414–1443), Chichele, did not hesitate, in 1427, to appeal to the council against a sentence pronounced upon him by Martin V.

Papal prestige was yet further weakened by the Renaissance disorders, and by the sixteenth century wars waged in Italy, in which the Popes had to take part on equal terms with petty temporal princes, exchanging the tiara for a helmet, like Julius II or, like Clement VII, casting themselves now into the emperor's arms, now into those of the King of France. In 1517 Pace, the Dean of St. Paul's, wrote a distressing account of the moral state of the Eternal City. . . . Ten years later, Rome was sacked by an unbridled and sacrilegious soldiery in the pay of the emperor, the Pope was imprisoned in the Castle St. Angelo, and Charles V declared that it was a just judgment of God. An ambassador of Charles V proposed to deprive the Pope of his temporal goods which, according to him, were the source of all the evil. The question was asked whether "the King of France would not create a patriarch in his own realm and renounce the obedience due to the Holy See, and whether the King of England and the other Christian princes would not follow this example." Wolsey, together with four other cardinals, protested, in the name of England and France, against any act which the Pope might perform during his captivity. He claimed to have the powers of a kind of vicar-general for the two countries. It was said that he was "going to France to separate the Churches of England and of France from that of Rome, not merely during the captivity of the Pope and to effect his liberation, but for a perpetual division," and some suggested to Charles V that, in order to avoid a schism, he should depose Clement VII and offer the tiara to Wolsey.

The subjection of the papacy to the King of France had brought about the Great Schism; its dependency upon the emperor might have equally disastrous results. The distrust which had taken hold of men's minds in 1527 persisted in England

---

[2] An enunciation of royal policy that violated ecclesiastical immunity to the advantage of the royal courts. The Constitutions were abandoned in the aftermath of Becket's murder.

[3] The various statutes prior to *praemunire* are doubtless meant here.

throughout the reign of Clement VII, and was easily fed. When Charles V begged the Pope to forbid the English Parliament to discuss the divorce there were very few Englishmen who were not openly indignant. More wounding still to national feeling was the summons issued to Henry to appear in Italy, a country dominated by the arms and influence of a foreign prince. "If his Grace" [the king], wrote Wolsey, "should come at any time to the Court of Rome, he would do the same with such a main and army royal as should be formidable to the Pope and to all Italy." And, in 1532, Henry told Francis I that if he went to Rome the Pope would soon be sorry he had summoned him. The nation was inclined to distrust a jurisdiction which was said to be influenced by her enemies.

Moreover, with the passing of time, the bonds uniting England and Rome had weakened. For four centuries there had been no English Pope, and the two setbacks Wolsey's hopes of the tiara had suffered, on the election of Adrian VI and Clement VII, made this exclusion more apparent. It was indeed customary to have an English cardinal in the Sacred College, but what is one cardinal in a body of between fifty and sixty members? England's share of influence in the great Christian council had therefore greatly decreased. Then again, the all-powerful Wolsey had secured his nomination for life as the legate of the Holy See . . . an office which he held from 1518 to 1529, and by holding it exercised unlimited authority over the clergy. The Church in England had but one link with Rome — its own legate; and when the one fell the other would fall too, as both Henry VIII and Anne Boleyn well knew. The nation became accustomed to this mediate jurisdiction, which was the first step towards a national Church. When, therefore, Henry VIII broke with Rome he was able to disguise the separation by giving to Cranmer the title of *legatus natus,* a title borne by the Archbishop of Canterbury in the twelfth century and one which, to the simple folk, might present the ap-

pearance of some vague bond between the Roman Church and the Church in England.

Finally, Rome's thunders were no longer able to shake the English nation. They had been used too frequently, especially in temporal matters, for Christian princes to have much fear of them. Charles V himself was scarcely moved by them. The excommunication of Henry VIII passed almost unnoticed. "The king," wrote the imperial ambassador, "said that he took no account of it, but made as great cheer as ever . . . for if the Pope issued 10,000 excommunications, he would not care a straw for them." And when the Holy See proposed to deprive Henry of his kingdom no one was willing to undertake the task. Although it concerned his aunt's honour, the emperor declined the offer. He would not even recall his ambassador from London, and was congratulated by his ministers because he had not to carry out the sentence against Henry. The era of the crusades was over, and national jealousies and political and commercial rivalries had superseded all ideas of chivalry. The helpless position of the Pope was clearly seen in the light of the apathy of the English and the political selfishness of other nations.

*   *   *

The anti-clerical feeling of part of the [English] population was reflected in Parliament, especially in the House of Commons, which was elected by the industrial and business classes, chafing, as usual, under the religious yoke and the ecclesiastical precepts. Wolsey dissolved the 1515 Parliament because of its attacks upon the clergy and, save in 1523, when the financial distress obliged him to do so, did not call a single Parliament together as long as he was in power, that is for nearly fifteen years. The Parliament which assembled after his downfall (November 1529) was not less advanced in its ideas than its predecessor in 1515: "My lords," Bishop Fisher exclaimed in the House of Lords, "you see clearly what bills come hither from the

Common House, and all is to the destruction of the Church. For God's sake, see what a realm the kingdom of Bohemia was, and when the Church went down, then fell the glory of the kingdom. Now, with the Commons is nothing but down with the Church!"

Even before Parliament met, the legate Campeggio had appealed to the king to uphold ecclesiastical liberty, which was threatened, and to prevent the destruction of the Church. He knew well what was in the minds of the country's representatives.

Parliament detested the clergy's privileges and began to attack them. John Taylor, who was a member both of Parliament and of Convocation, observed in 1515 that "in Convocation and in Parliament very dangerous dissensions arose between the clergy and the secular power on the subject of the Church's liberties."

Parliament interfered in the administration of the sacraments and in ecclesiastical burials. In 1512 it took the "privilege of the clergy" (which meant exemption from royal jurisdiction) from all clerics, not yet sub-deacons, who were accused of murder or felony. The Abbot of Winchcombe protested against this law in the name of the Church's liberties, whereas Standish, guardian of the Franciscan convent in London, upheld and approved it. The secular peers demanded that the prelates should make the abbot withdraw his words. As Standish had been summoned by the Convocation of 1515 to explain his conduct, the judges to whom he appealed declared that all who had taken proceedings against him were subject to the penalties of *praemunire*. Pace says that he won favour with all the courtiers, he became a favourite at Court and was soon made Bishop of St. Asaph (1518).

Parliament had scarcely been recalled from the long rest to which Wolsey had relegated it before it resumed the work begun in the first years of Henry's reign. At that time the Duke of Norfolk wrote: "Notwithstanding the infinite clamours of the temporality here in parliament against the misuse of the spiritual jurisdiction, the king will stop all evil effects if the Pope does not handle him unkindly. This realm did never grudge the tenth part against the abuses of the Church at no parliament in my days as they do now."

Fresh attacks were made upon the immunities of the clergy and upon the ecclesiastical courts. The latter were blamed for being so expensive, for their endless delays, and for the manner in which they condemned poor people either to abjure or else to burn at the stake, without allowing them any witnesses. The House of Commons complained that the clergy in Convocation issued precepts which were incompatible with the laws of the realm, that benefices were given to minors, that churchmen were taking up secular employment, and that there were too many festivals, especially in the autumn. They wanted to forbid monks to have anything to do with industry or business, and rectors and bishops' administrators to possess farms. In 1532 they were doubtful about voting the suppression of the annates because they could not see any advantage in relieving the bishops of this tax.

These ill-feelings, grievances, and jealousies against the clergy and their privileges had long been festering in the minds of a certain class of Englishmen. To say that the Parliament which sat from 1529 to 1536 and which was responsible for the breach with Rome acted only under pressure from the king would be, to put it mildly, an exaggeration. The Bills proposed in 1530 and 1531 were merely a repetition or a consequence of the recriminations made in 1515. Why should Wolsey have dissolved and then ceased altogether to convoke Parliament, if it had been so easy to manage and if the anti-clerical prejudices were merely artificial? Why were the Commons, at the time of the divorce, so ready and so willing to pass Bills for the subjection of the clergy, whereas they absolutely refused, with one exception, to vote for any fresh subsidies or taxes, or expenditure on armaments? Neither would they pass the Act on "Uses and Wills," for which the king had asked so often in order to make his feudal rights secure;[4] yet the Lords had accepted it (1532) and there was nothing that the king desired more. "The demand," Chapuys observed, "has been the occasion of strange words against the king and council. Nothing has been concluded." "Henry," he wrote again, "has been trying to obtain from parliament the grant of a third of the feudal property of deceased lords, but as yet has got nothing." More than one Bill presented by the government in 1534 was rejected or altered, and the Parliament of 1545, which is supposed to have been the most servile of the whole of this reign, made great difficulties about accepting certain Bills, and passed others which the king had to veto. If then Parliament threw out some of the king's proposals, may we not conclude that it could have rejected others, too, had it wished so to do?

Liberty of speech was enjoyed by all. In the House of Lords the Bishops of St. Asaph and Bath attacked the speeches made by their episcopal brethren of Lincoln and London in favour of the divorce (1531), and a member of the House of Commons, Temse, did not hesitate to tell the king that he ought to take his wife back again (May 1532). There was nothing the king would feel more than that. "There was great murmuring among them in the Chamber of the Commons," wrote Chapuys in 1531, "where it was publicly said in the presence of some of the Privy Council that the king had burdened and oppressed the kingdom with more imposts and exactions than any three or four of his predecessors, and he ought to consider that the strength of the king lay in the affections of his people."

After Henry's death (1547) Bishop Gardiner regretfully recalled the days when men could speak freely in Parliament without having anything to fear. In 1515 the clergy begged the king to grant them the same freedom in Convocation as was enjoyed in Parliament, where members might attack the laws of the country with impunity.

The Bills laid before Parliament were carefully revised, and sometimes completely altered by the two Houses, as we can see by the rough drafts which have come down to us. It was not therefore simply a case of writing them in the Statute Book. It cannot be said that because most of these Bills came from the government itself the two Houses were servile, for this was the ordinary mode of procedure, and it still obtains. The theory that Parliament exists only to make its own laws was applied in England only when there was radical opposition between the legislative and executive powers. Certain Bills are to be found which were corrected by Cromwell or by one of the king's clerks; but it does not follow that because nine-tenths of modern legislation is drawn up by parliamentary clerks that such legislation is against popular opinion.

Henry VIII possessed a real advantage in the fact that members of Parliament in the sixteenth century were representatives, and not delegates as at the present day. They had received no imperative mandate from the people, and could therefore be more easily moved by exterior circumstances, such as a speech, or fear of the king, or other similar motives.

There was more freedom at the elections than has been asserted. Thus the London elections of 1529 were carried out according to the laws laid down, *immensa communitate tunc praesente*.[5] The government was always careful not to alienate the liberty which the counties enjoyed, and practically the only places where it could exercise any influence were the very limited number of royal boroughs; no attempt was made to increase the number of these until after 1529. It was not till later that the government systematically intervened in

---

[4] Landed families often placed encumbrances upon estates in order to avoid the Crown's managerial and fiscal prerogatives, especially wardship (guardian rights over minors who were heirs to land held in military tenure) and its incidents.

[5] "With the greatest part of the community being present."

the elections. This move was due to Thomas Cromwell, who wanted to make sure that he would have a majority; but he himself fell shortly afterwards. The purifying of the English Parliament was, generally speaking, the death agony of a dying government. Henry VIII had a greater influence in the House of Lords, where he could create new peers, than in the House of Commons. Most of the peers at the end of his reign owed their existence to him; for the Wars of the Roses had long ago caused the disappearance of the lords who might have resisted the Crown.

The electors themselves, without the slightest intervention of the Crown, constituted the House of Commons as the king desired. In the country districts, where the franchise was given only to freeholders of property valued at forty shillings, parliamentary members were drawn from the gentry, and in the towns, where there were no longer any democratic pretensions, from the rich merchants. Now these two classes were the strongest supporters the Tudors had, just as to-day they uphold the government and the Anglican Church. They upheld Henry VIII's policy as much as any royal officials would have done, because the king and they had interests in common. To support Henry's secular politics was the only way to avoid civil war and the consequent harm it would do to public prosperity; and in matters of ecclesiastical policy both the gentry and the merchants agreed with the king that the clergy had too many privileges and too much wealth, and that in their own hands this wealth might be used to greater advantage. Hence Henry and his Parliament were perfectly in accord in their views. Brewer[6] observes that Parliament "faithfully reflected the king's wishes and his policy." Parliament and the king were close allies in their fight against all rival jurisdictions, and it was to the advantage of each party to increase the

power of the other. The laws passed in the second half of this reign bear testimony to this. Their common interests produced harmony of action.

Dogma, in fact, did not have the same share in the Reformation in England as did justification by faith in Germany, or predestination in Switzerland. Englishmen are not lovers of abstract ideas. Not being logical like the French, nor mystics like the Germans, they do not enter into theological quarrels; they are more for questions of a practical nature. So the Reformation began in England, not with the proclamation of some theological novelty, but rather with the destroying of the clergy's privileges and confiscation of the Church's property. The Reformation in this country was brought about solely by a grievance of a practical order intimately bound up with a question of money. "At the beginning, the apostles left their fishing of fishes, and became fishers of men; and now we, which talk much of Christ and his holy word, have, I fear me, used a much contrary way, for we leave fishing for men, and fish again in the tempestuous seas of this world for gain and wicked mammon."

All Henry had to do was to fan the passions of Parliament and thus secure an instrument by which he could dominate and govern. There was no need to enslave it, he simply let it have the reins. He took good care not to dissolve Parliament, for in his hands it was another Ulysses' bow which he alone could bend. On November 3rd, 1529, Parliament met at Westminster. It was not dissolved until the last link of the chain binding the Church in England to Rome had been severed, and the country had been plunged into that sixty years' conflict which ended only with the defeat of the invincible Armada. Parliament was aiming less at Rome than at the Church, whose privileges it hated and whose property it envied, but in striking at one it hit the other. In depriving the clergy of their independence and making them wholly subject to the king, it automatically removed them from papal jurisdiction.

[6] John Sharon Brewer, first editor of the vast *Letter and Papers . . . of the Reign of Henry VIII* and the author of two volumes on the years 1509–30.

The brac h[7] with Rome was not, in fact, a spontaneous movement of the church in England. It was not the rejection of a yoke which would have burdened it. In Convocation the Church adopted a purely defensive attitude. The clergy suggested no innovations; they would have been glad to be out of it all. Resistance may possibly have been their only chance, but England no longer possessed a Thomas à Becket or a Winchelsey,[8] and the sole excuse their successor in the primatial see of Canterbury, Warham, could find for his compliance was the words of Holy Writ: *Ira principis mors est,*[9] and we shall see the sorry part the Convocations played.

The Reformation in England, then, was wrought by agreement, by the combined action of Parliament and the king, but Henry's was the larger share. It is true he did not create the factors of this religious revolution, but he used them with a coolness and calculation worthy of Machiavelli's *Prince*. He turned the needs of his people, their passions and grievances, and even their national spirit to his own advantage; everything had to fit in with his own plans. No matter how pressing Parliament might have been, the king could have decided in favour of the Church by ranging himself on her side. Before leaving England, Campeggio besought him to do so.

In Henry IV's time the gentry and the temporal lords had also demanded the secularization of Church property, and Wiclif had called upon the civil powers to reform the Church. But the king upheld the Church then because he needed her help to make his crown secure, and so nothing was changed. Great revolutions depend upon a number of causes acting simultaneously, and often fail because one cause is defective. The defective cause in the Lancastrian period was the king himself. It was not so in the period with which we are concerned, not because Henry VIII had any leanings towards novelties — he maintained the orthodox teaching — not because Rome's yoke weighed him down — until then he had been perfectly in accord with the Holy See, which had given him his title *Defensor fidei* — but because he wanted the Pope to divorce him from Catherine of Aragon. Clement VII's opposition threw Henry on the side which was hostile to the Church, and turned the tide in favour of schism. Hence the historical importance of Henry VIII's divorce is not that it was one of the causes in itself, but that by converting into enmity a former friendship it alienated from Rome the only power capable of keeping together the forces that were working against the Church and tending to rend it asunder.

[7] Thus in the original; read either "break" or "breach."

[8] Robert Winchelsey, Archbishop of Canterbury (1293–1313), an exponent of the priority of the English churchman's allegiance to Pope Boniface VIII as against that owed to King Edward I.

[9] "The anger of the king is death."

TUDOR HUMANISM AND HENRY VIII

DOUGLAS BUSH

Harvard's Gurney Professor of English Literature Emeritus ranks as one of the foremost scholars of Renaissance English letters and thought. Born and educated in Canada, Douglas Bush came to the United States as a teacher in 1924; from 1936 until his retirement in 1966 he taught at Harvard. The recipient of a Guggenheim Fellowship and honorary Litt.D. degrees from nearly a dozen colleges and universities, Professor Bush has distinguished himself as an editor (Milton, Keats, Tennyson) and as the author of numerous major books of a critical and synthetic nature. His important works include *Mythology and the Renaissance Tradition in English Poetry; The Renaissance and English Humanism; John Milton;* and *English Literature in the Earlier Seventeenth Century, 1600–1660.*

IN HIS ADMIRABLE *Thomas More,* Professor R. W. Chambers pillories Henry VIII as the ruthless destroyer of the rich culture which England possessed at the opening of the sixteenth century. He makes his own the argument put forth by J. S. Phillimore in what he calls "a vital essay, to which every student of More is under a heavy debt." Phillimore's thesis was "that the Humanist Movement in England was arrested at the middle of the sixteenth century and did not mature till more than a century later; that the movement was typically personified in More; and that his death was the blow which paralysed it." Mr. Chambers elaborates "the story of arrest and frustration" in this manner:

The poets flocked to Henry's court; he stopped their music, and for a generation after the execution of Surrey there is nothing worth notice, save the sombre poems in which Sackville, before turning away from poetry, lamented that eminence led only to destruction. In the ordinary course, Surrey might have lived another thirty or forty years, the centre of a circle of court poets. As it is, the history of the sonnet in England is a blank between 1547 and about 1580, and English poetry as a whole is negligible till it begins its magnificent progress again with Spenser and Sidney. Prose had a similar set-back. After the generation of Tyndale and Coverdale, Fisher and More and his school, there is no eminence till we come to Hooker and Bacon — a gap of more than a generation. Contemporaries noticed the gap, and wondered that More's example had not proved more fruitful. In the field of scholarship Henry's achievement was really remarkable. There were four great international scholars, and, in England, two great patrons of learning. Of the six, Henry cold-shouldered Erasmus out of England, imprisoned Vives, decapitated More and Fisher, and frightened Wolsey to death. "Had Erasmus, instead of being an honoured guest at Rome, at Paris, or in the States of the Empire, been beheaded by Charles V or Francis I, all learning would have felt the blow, and shrunk." In England, all learning felt the blow, and shrank. It was not till the days of Bentley[1] that classical scholarship recovered in England the position it held in the days of Erasmus,

[1] The reference is to Richard Bentley (1662–1742), Master of Trinity College, Cambridge, 1700–1742, a great classical scholar, editor of Homer, Horace, and Milton.

From Douglas Bush, "Tudor Humanism and Henry VIII," *University of Toronto Quarterly,* VII (1938), pp. 162–77. Reprinted by permission of the University of Toronto Press, Douglas Bush, and the *University of Toronto Quarterly.*

before Henry axed it. To the Universities, Henry's spoliation meant a loss, for which the foundation of a few Readerships offered small compensation. In 1550 Latimer writes, "It would pity a man's heart to hear that, that I hear of the state of Cambridge. . . . I think there be at this day ten thousand students less than were within these twenty years, and fewer preachers." As to the grammar schools, More's school of St. Antony was only one of a vast number which withered away.

In a brief survey of a complex problem I must pass by many topics that Mr. Chambers touches. The lack of good poets in the middle of the century, for instance, might be charged against God rather than against his royal representative, for there are many ages of peace and plenty in which good poets simply do not happen to be born. As for a blank in the history of the sonnet between 1547 and 1580, if Henry was responsible for that it ought to be listed along with the royal navy as one of his major achievements; one could almost wish the blank had lasted twenty years longer. And, in spite of Mr. Chambers's notable study of early English prose, one is bewildered by the critical judgment which finds no eminence in prose between More's time and Hooker and Bacon. Is there no eminence in the *Book of Common Prayer*, in North's *Plutarch*,[2] in Sidney's *Defence of Poesy*,[3] in Hakluyt's *Voyages*,[4] not to mention such lesser but able prosemen as Ascham, Hoby, Richard Eden, and others?[5]

But our concern here is with humanism in its special sense, and with the theory that it was paralysed by the execution of More. The proponents of this view give small evidence that the execution of the lord chancellor of England was felt as a blow to learning; they only feel that that must have been the effect. But, granted for the moment that the arrest of humanism was as complete as these scholars allege, there were far too many factors involved to permit any such simple explanation. I cannot find reason to suppose that the course of Tudor humanism would have been very different from what it was if More and Fisher had never been executed. To say that is not, of course, to slight the great service that both men, especially Fisher, did to learning.

For the main cause of the setback to learning in the universities, one has only to recall the conditions in which scholars were living. In the twenty-five years from 1535 to 1560, the official religion of the country changed four times, from papal to non-papal Catholicism, from that to Protestantism, from Protestantism to papal Catholicism, and from that to Protestantism again. The university men who lived through this period were, of course, at the centre of religious and political controversy and were subjected, directly or indirectly, to successive and conflicting religious tests. And no sooner had the Elizabethan settlement been reached than strife between Anglican and Puritan commenced. From looking abroad at the present time we know how difficult it is for disinterested learning to flourish when scholars have lost their consciousness of freedom and security. In the middle of the sixteenth century there were keener anxieties than that — the fear of eating mice at Zürich, or much worse, of imprisonment and death. Ascham, thanks largely to the Catholic Gardiner, weathered the storms, but he had some unhappy years. Cheke[6] ended his life miserably with exile, imprisonment, and recantation. Henry VIII was responsible for only the beginning of these troubles, and the later burning of Latimer,[7]

[2] Sir Thomas North; his translation of Plutarch's *Lives* was Shakespeare's storehouse.

[3] Sir Philip Sidney, the great poet and courtier.

[4] Richard Hakluyt (?1552–1616), geographer and propagandist of English expansion.

[5] Roger Ascham, whose *Scholemaster* is justly famous; Sir Thomas Hoby, the translator of Castiglione's *Courtier* and Martin Bucer's *Gratulation*; Richard Eden, translator of works in science and cosmography and the publisher of *The Decades of the New Worlde, or West India in 1555* — a work of great influence on English thought about America.

[6] Sir John Cheke, leader of Greek scholars at Cambridge and an active Protestant politician.

[7] Hugh Latimer, Protestant divine and celebrated preacher.

Ridley,[8] and Cranmer at Oxford may appear to have been a much greater and more direct blow to learning than the execution of More. Apart from such eminent victims, the history of most of the colleges throughout the period reveals continual disturbance and continual changing of masters, according as the reforming or the conservative party got the upper hand. And there was a vast amount of ecclesiastical controversy, ranging from Henry's divorce to the Eucharist. Amid such unrest, such vicissitudes, and such polemics, the wonder is that humanism did not suffer far more than it did.

*   *   *

Men's vision was strongly coloured by religious and political as well as personal prejudice. Further, like academic men in all ages, they were much given to hasty expressions of rhetorical pessimism. There was disagreement not only between Protestants and Catholics but among Protestants as to the nature and causes of the decline in learning; a main theme on both sides was the fear of an inadequate supply of learned clergy. . . . In that respect the decline seems to have been much exaggerated. The more important and difficult question of a decline in morale we have partly touched, and here too we may think the case somewhat overdrawn, though at best it was serious enough.

In this brief sketch of the educational problem something has been said incidentally in defence of Henry VIII. . . . We have observed his founding or refounding of important schools and colleges. He seriously desired to provide a supply of educated men for the service of state and church, and one piece of evidence is the establishment of scholarships. In 1536 a royal injunction required every priest with emoluments of one hundred pounds or more to maintain a scholar at a university or grammar school. We do not know how effective this rule was, but it may be supposed to have worked pretty well, since it

was re-enacted under Edward and again under Elizabeth. One minor but not insignificant advance was the authorization of what was called Lily's *Grammar*[9] as the text-book in all grammar schools.

For further evidence of Henry's support of education and the new learning one may quote the injunctions to Cambridge of 1535. "He inciteth them to the study of tongues. . . . He enjoineth them to found, on the joint cost of all the Colleges, two Lectures, the one of Latin, the other of Greek, to be daily read, (and, by consequence, heard), on great penalties." Duns Scotus and his tribe are banished, along with canon law, and in their place is required the study of Aristotle, Rudolph Agricola,[10] Melanchthon, and others. The "Master of the Sentences" is to give way to the Bible. Mr. Chambers's sniff at Henry's few readerships presumably includes not only the lectureships just mentioned but the Regius Professorships founded at Cambridge and Oxford, which from the first had some distinguished incumbents and greatly stimulated learning in Greek, Hebrew, Civil Law, Medicine, and Theology. In regard to all these reforms it may be said that Henry himself was not bearing the cost, or that the ideas were not original with him. To frame an answer on the lowest possible level, one may say first, according to an ancient proverb, that a thief gives all he does not take, and, secondly, on the same principle, that a ruler deserves credit for all the acts he does not veto.

Let us recall the Phillimore-Chambers theory of the effect of More's execution: "In England, all learning felt the blow, and shrank. It was not till the days of Bentley that classical scholarship recovered in England the position it held in the days of Erasmus, before Henry axed it." Erasmus' teaching of Greek at Cambridge in 1511–4 may have given a great impetus to the English Reformation, but in the matter of Greek scholarship it was a sad disillusion-

---

[8] Nicholas Ridley, another Cambridge Protestant divine and, like Latimer, a bishop.

[9] William Lily's *Grammatices Rudimenta* was first published in 1527, after Lily's death.

[10] The very famous Dutch humanist and teacher.

ment for the teacher. Greek did not really begin at Cambridge until 1518, when Richard Croke was brought, under Henry's auspices, from an illustrious professorship at Leipsig. Henry was not responsible for the prolonged hostility to Greek which broke out in the "Trojan" war at Oxford in the same year.[11] Nor did Henry dictate Gardiner's fierce and repeated decrees against the reformed pronunciation of Greek inaugurated by Smith[12] and Cheke, decrees which, said Ascham in his impetuous way, almost extinguished all zeal for learning in Cambridge. In these things, and in others which must be passed by, we have, not at all the effect of More's execution, but the bitter antagonism of Catholic adherents of the old learning, whose attitude toward Greek and humanism was generally very different from More's. The reactionaries would have kept the universities tied to degenerate scholasticism if it had not been for a few powerful supporters of humanism, and, though full honour is due to such men as Fisher and Fox, the dominant factor was that Henry was on the side of the new learning.

We might name an unbroken succession of eminent classical scholars throughout the long blank period that Mr. Chambers deplores, but we can glance at only the beginning of it, say the dozen years following the death of More, when the paralysis of humanism might be supposed to be at its worst. And as soon as we look at those years, we realize that we are considering the one period in English history before Bentley when classical studies in an English university were a matter of international fame, when Sir John Cheke taught Cambridge and King Edward Greek. At Cambridge, in this period of arrested humanism, we have, in addition to Cheke and Sir Thomas Smith, both Regius Professors, Ascham himself, William Grindall, Wil-

liam Cecil, Thomas Watson, James Pilkington, and William Bill. Of these men all but Smith were at St. John's. Among other notable scholars in the two universities were Walter Haddon, John Ponet, John Redman, Robert Pember, John Caius, Thomas Wilson, Nicholas Carr, Nicholas Ridley, John Aylmer, Matthew Parker.[13] Nearly all these men were Protestants. Catholics were not paralysed by the death of More; they were in general, as I said, exponents of the old learning, even when, as in some cases, they were not unfriendly to the new. Here we might recall that young friend of More, Thomas Lupset,[14] who would have been an ornament of this age if he had not died in early manhood. And, though he was not an academic man, one should name Sir Thomas Elyot, one of the most authentic humanists of the century. Of these names many, of course, mean little now except to scholars, but in their day — or should one say in their night? — they were bright beacons, and a respectable number of them are important still. Among the successors of Colet and More one could not ask for better exemplars of Christian humanism than Cheke and Ascham. That the later pair are of smaller stature Phillimore and Chambers would perhaps explain by saying (after *1066 and All That*) that they were not angels but Anglicans.

One general point urged by Phillimore, and at least implied by Mr. Chambers, seems to me fundamental. No Tudor classical scholar, says Phillimore, can be compared for a moment with Lambin and Turnèbe;[15] classical scholarship in England, say both men, did not recover itself until

[13] Cecil was more famous as a Secretary of State, Lord Treasurer, and diplomat under Elizabeth. Parker was the Queen's great Archbishop of Canterbury.

[14] Lupset edited Galen and helped More, Erasmus, and Linacre to prepare works for the press.

[15] Denys Lambin and Adrien Turnèbe, both professors of Greek at Paris in the mid-sixteenth century. Lambin made his mark in Latin editions of Plautus, Lucretius, Horace, and Cicero, however. Turnèbe brought out brilliant texts of Philo, Sophocles, and Aeschylus.

[11] This is a reference to the anti-Greek faction of clerics among the Oxford dons.

[12] Sir Thomas Smith, scholar and Secretary of State to Edward VI; in exile under Mary but active in politics and diplomacy under Elizabeth I.

the days of Bentley. In other words, the failure in England to produce any great works of pure scholarship is a mark of arrested development. So far as the humanists were drawn into ecclesiastical controversy, we may regret the conditions which fostered much vain writing and speaking, but otherwise the notion of arrested development betrays a misunderstanding of the vital spirit of English humanism. Of course a number of the humanists wrote little or nothing because, like the fifteenth-century humanists before them, they were busy academic and ecclesiastical administrators — or perhaps they seemed busier than they were. Moreover, the mere burden of teaching borne by such men as Cheke was far greater than that of modern professors. But the real truth lies much deeper than these external circumstances, and it is strange that Phillimore and Mr. Chambers, in contemplating their idol, should not have been saved from an obvious fallacy. More did not seek to rival Scaliger,[16] nor did Erasmus envy the reputation of Budé.[17] Erasmus and More did not investigate the coinage or the grammar of the ancients; they sought to make the rational wisdom of antiquity supplement the teaching of Christ. "You," wrote Erasmus to Budé, "have preferred to be understood by the learned, I, if I can, by the many; your aim is to conquer, mine to teach or persuade." The main impulse of Tudor humanism, and of the best continental humanism, was not that life should be given up to classical learning, but that classical learning should be an aid to the active Christian life. *The Praise of Folly* and *Utopia, The Governour* and *The Schoolmaster,* remain living books. Who except the scholar has heard of Lambin and Turnèbe, and how many scholars could say fifty words about either? I am not disparaging the work of these and other men who did so much to enlarge and purify classical learning, but we should never forget that the purpose of Tudor humanism was education. The broad aim was training in virtue and good letters, the special aim was preparing young men for public life. It was these Tudor humanists who established what was to remain the ruling motive of English classical study down to the days of "the Jowett mind."[18] Would it have been better that William Cecil should continue as a classical don, and perhaps crown his life with an edition of Aristotle's *Politics,* than that he should apply ancient wisdom to practical statesmanship — not without help from Machiavelli? Classical scholars, poor and simple, have always been rare accidents in England. For scholarship means discovery, humanism means discipline. A. E. Housman (like Bentley) believed that the function of a classical scholar in these times was the emending of texts, preferably those of bad poets. Erasmus and More, and Cheke and Ascham and Smith, would have given their approval to Sir Alfred Zimmern and Professor Gilbert Murray for working at Geneva....[19]

Renaissance humanism did not rise, as is commonly said, in opposition to theology and religion; it rose mainly in opposition to irreligious and "unhuman" science and philosophy. It strove, as so many movements have striven, to reassert human values, which meant also divine values, against barren logic or a philosophy of nature which neglected the truly human and divine.

[16] Joseph Scaliger (1540–1609) is perhaps the greatest name in the history of classical scholarship; he is primarily remembered as the editor of the Latin elegiac poets Catullus, Tibullus, and Propertius, and as the author of a critical work on ancient chronology which founded modern historical studies of its kind (*De Emendatione temporum*).

[17] Guillaume Budé, an early sixteenth-century classicist and political thinker who specialized in studies of Greek law and language.

[18] Benjamin Jowett (1817–93), translator of Plato and famed Master of Balliol, Oxford, who also worked extensively on scriptural translations (very liberal), Thucydides, and Aristotle.

[19] Zimmern and Murray: the one a student of Greek political life and the other of Greek drama; both active in the League of Nations.

KING OR MINISTER?

G. R. ELTON

G. R. Elton was born in 1921. After coming to England from Prague, he began historical studies and took a Ph.D. at University College, London. Since 1948 he has established himself as a leading authority on the Tudor period, especially on constitutional matters relating to the Reformation. He is currently Professor of Constitutional History in Cambridge University and a fellow of Clare College. Among his many provocative articles and books the most important are his *The Tudor Revolution in Government* and *The Tudor Constitution*. Among his other works *Star Chamber Stories* provides unique insights into the impact of government on Englishmen of every rank and station. His interests in the Reformation period outside of England are illustrated in his editorship of Volume Two of the *New Cambridge Modern History* and the brilliant feat of compression entitled *Reformation Europe, 1517–1559*.

THE QUESTION whether Henry VIII or Thomas Cromwell supplied the ideas and the policy which underlay the break with Rome is of more interest than may be imagined. Until it is answered neither the men nor the event can really be understood. The English Reformation gave to England, the English monarchy, and the English church a character quite their own: this makes it important to know just how and why and through whom it happened. It may perhaps be thought strange that so well-worked a part of English history should be supposed to retain some mysteries still. . . . On the face of it, a new study of those critical years in the 1530's might, to say the least, not be without reward. Here I shall attempt only to elucidate the true relationship between the two leading personalities of that age, for the prevailing notions seem to me to do scant justice to the genius of the minister and vastly to overrate the genius of the king. One's opinion of Henry VIII must stand by one's view of his part in the Reformation. The positive achievements of his long reign were crowded into its middle years; if he deserves the high opinion of his skill and understanding which so many moderns seem to hold it must be because he was "the architect of the Reformation." But whether he was that remains to be seen.

Since it is the purpose of this paper to set up Thomas Cromwell as the moving spirit in the early Reformation, it will be of assistance to recall that this view is far from original. It was held, to begin with, by some of Cromwell's contemporaries — by Cardinal Pole, for instance, by the imperial ambassador Eustace Chapuys, and by John Foxe.[1] It was adopted outright — mainly in reliance on Pole and without proper investigation — by many nineteenth-century historians. But then came Pollard, who held that the Reformation was a natural development from discoverable causes which was given its particular direction by the king himself; and he had the support of the other early-Tudor pundit of the day, Gaird-

[1] The Protestant martyrologist (*Acts and Monuments*, more familiarly Foxe's *Book of Martyrs*).

From G. R. Elton, "King or Minister? The Man Behind the Henrician Reformation," *History*, XXXIX (1954), pp. 216–32. Reprinted by permission of the author, and the editor of *History*, Professor Alfred Cobban.

ner,[2] who ascribed to Cromwell at best out-
standing executive skill with perhaps some
independent advice. . . . In tilting at Pollard — with all the deference due to so great
a historian and fully conscious of my temer-
ity in attacking one of his fundamental
tenets — I am not, therefore, altogether
without company both past and present.

It is time to turn from what has been
said about Cromwell and Henry to what
can be found in the evidence. Is it, in fact,
possible to come to conclusions in this matter which are more than opinions? Can one
decide with any degree of certainty whether
Thomas Cromwell or Henry VIII evolved
the plan which led to the schism and the
establishment of the royal supremacy, especially since both men must have worked
together and much of the story must lie
for ever hidden in unrecorded conversa-
tions, council meetings, and even private
thoughts? I believe that despite these obstacles an answer is possible. In the first place,
we can investigate the relations between
king and minister to see whether they permit an insight into their position towards
each other. Secondly, a re-interpretation
of the course of the Henrician Reformation
collated with Cromwell's career will, it is
hoped, offer a solution of the problem.

No attempt to ignore or despise Henry
VIII could ever be successful. Whatever
may be thought of his character, he dominated the history of his time: he was a
mighty king, no man's puppet, and never
ignorant of what was done in his name.
He took much active interest in the run-
ning of the realm, decided what policy was
to be followed, made and unmade ministers
and servants, and kept in his head and
hand the strings of government. To suppose that Cromwell's was the real mind
behind the great revolution is not to suppose that Henry had no mind at all. But
the events of the reign — its confusion, its
changing character, Henry's dependence
on ministers, and so forth — all go to show
that his was definitely an unoriginal and
unproductive mind, intelligent indeed and
capable of the swift assimilation of ideas,
but unable to penetrate independently to
the heart of a problem and its solution.
Henry had the qualities of a first-rate politician — especially a remarkable opportun-
ism — without the equipment of a first-rate
statesman. Moreover, he was lazy: he took
little part in the detailed business of government and surrendered the kind of prime-
ministerial position which Henry VII had
occupied. Between them, his unoriginality
and his laziness made him less really decisive than his personality and the deference
of others would suggest. For the king's part
in government is the harder to assess because his servants constantly protested that
they were merely carrying out his orders.
. . . We must never be so simple as to
accept unquestioningly some Tudor politician's statement that he had his sovereign's
orders for his doings, even as we must not
be so subtle as always to disbelieve him.
Sixteenth-century ministers did not proclaim their independence of the crown, but
their prudent citation of authority is not
proof that they were not after all acting on
their own initiative.

Cromwell's relations with Henry are the
more obscured by this difficulty because
Cromwell was normally careful to give no
grounds for such accusations of independent action as had helped to bring Wolsey
low. Instead he cultivated a sedulous obsequiousness in his letters to the king which
contrasts strongly with his upright and
straightforward address to all others. Advice
which would involve the king in doing
some work he wrapped up in apologies for
his "bold audacite." Though he had the
king's ear, he knew Henry well enough to
disclaim all ability to rule the king's wishes.
. . . He had no illusions about a favour
which could never be taken for granted; in
April 1536 he commented to Chapuys with
unusual frankness on the mutability of
things of which, he said, he had had a recent "domestic" example in the fall of Anne
Boleyn. Henry VIII was hard to manage,
as Wolsey's successors discovered before

---

[2] James Gairdner, who succeeded J. S. Brewer as
editor of *Letter and Papers . . . of Henry VIII*, an
ardent partisan of Wolsey and the author or editor
of many books on Tudor history.

they learned how to do business with him. Great care was the more necessary because his reliance on others might at any moment give place to personal intervention. He surrendered his kingship to nobody.

However, that the whole truth does not lie in this picture of an active king to whom all things are deferred is sufficiently indicated in Cromwell's own correspondence. He summarized letters from abroad because they were too "long and diffuse" to trouble the king with; he habitually drafted the instructions and other state papers which the king simply accepted by signing them; he interviewed ambassadors and conducted most of the negotiations. He could act without specific authority, as when he "thought better" to send instructions "by my priuate letters then to put your highnes to the payne to have written and troubled your self with thesame," a delicate way of excusing his omission to apply for orders. In April 1539, ill with fever, he recited a long list of things done on his own responsibility which would ordinarily exhaust the energies of a man in the best of health. Writing from the Tower after his fall, he summed up his essential liberty of action:

I haue medelyd in So many matyers vinder your Highnes that I am not hable to answer them all . . . but harde it ys for me or any other medlyng as I haue done to lyue vnder your grace and your lawse but we must daylye offende.

Unless we wish to suppose that Cromwell meant to accuse the king of authorizing breaches of the law — and of course he did not — it follows that he was accusing himself of often acting in affairs of state without the king's knowledge or authority.

The question here is whether it was Cromwell's mind or Henry's that evolved the plan for breaking the deadlock created by Wolsey's failure to get the king his divorce. What has been shown so far is that there is no justification for the frequent assertion that Cromwell was a mere "instrument," in government and affairs he followed his own mind. But while this makes it possible to see in him the maker of the

Reformation if further proof is forthcoming, it does not do so by itself. The answer can only be found in a re-interpretation of the meaning, and especially of the chronology, of the Henrician Reformation.

The whole interpretation depends on chronology because Cromwell did not immediately succeed Wolsey as the king's chief minister. If he represented a policy of his own one might expect to see it appear with his arrival in power in 1532; and this is what happened. It is necessary to keep in mind what the "Henrician Reformation" really meant: the break with Rome — the withdrawal from the papal obedience — the creation of a schismatic English church — the setting up of the royal supremacy. All these are different, and in part tendentious, descriptions of one thing: the definition of independent national sovereignty achieved by the destruction of the papal jurisdiction in England. There lay the supremely important constitutional achievement of the 1530's. It came about because of the king's desire for a divorce from his first wife; it was greatly facilitated by the dislike of clergy and papacy which prevailed among the English laity; it may even have been assisted by the supposed spread of new and reformist ideas, whether Lutheran or humanist, though here the present writer would advocate the utmost caution. But in none of these things lay the essence of the change. Henry's campaign to have his marriage annulled is one thing; his break with the pope is another. The break was the means by which in the end the marriage was annulled; but Henry tried other means, and the historical importance of the break did not consist even mainly in the accomplishment of the divorce. To understand the years 1527–34 one must indeed start from the divorce, but one must try to follow events without allowing one's knowledge of the outcome to influence interpretation. One must attempt to discover what the king was up to as time went on.

This goes counter to Pollard's view that "the general course of the Reformation was a perfectly natural development from existing circumstances which it is idle to attribute to the influence of any one man." It was his opinion that Henry knew from the beginning where he was heading, though he had hopes that he would not be driven all the way but might compel the pope to surrender before the break came. In Pollard's own metaphor, the outworks were sapped and the fortress taken step by predetermined step. . . . This I believe to be now the accepted view: it credits the king both with farsighted plans and with an immediate ready radicalism of action. But it cannot be reconciled with those six long and tiresome years spent over the business. . . . This view makes better sense. Unable to see how he could legitimately marry Anne without the pope's connivance, and unaware of the possible implications of a royal supremacy in the church, Henry did not at first plan anything as extreme as a break with Rome. The ideas on which the revolution rested only appeared in the course of time.

To make the disagreement plain: Pollard held that a policy which relied on bringing Clement VII to compliance was the natural preliminary to a policy which solved the problem by ignoring the pope altogether. Put like this, it surely looks as though there were two radically different lines of approach rather than one naturally developing single line. With dubious logic, Pollard argued that the ultimate outcome, being inevitable (which one may doubt), was therefore envisaged from the first. What proof is offered? The Reformation was "so far dictated by circumstances that intelligent observers could predict its general tenor" even before November 1529. "General tenor" is a question-begging phrase; of course, intelligent observers could foresee some of the issues that were going to be raised, but did they forecast, and did Henry show signs of aiming at, something very like the royal supremacy and break with Rome ultimately established? The alleged evidence — commonly cited from a calendar which at times mistranslates tendentiously — will not bear this out. There is Cam-

peggio's report in October 1529 of Wolsey's warning that failure to give the king his divorce would result in the ruin of the realm, of Wolsey, and of the reputation of the church in England. He cited Germany to show what a cardinal's intransigence could do and repeatedly asserted that this would shatter the authority of the Apostolic See which he had served so well and with which all his greatness was linked. . . . He thought, in fact, only that ecclesiastical influence would decline; there is nothing to prove that he ever considered the likelihood of England breaking all ties with Rome.

Nor is the proof to be found in the reports of various French envoys, especially Jean du Bellay, Bishop of Bayonne, who was in England in 1529. He wrote in August that parliament would meet in winter and that then "they would act of their own unfettered power" if the pope failed to oblige. . . . Of course, everyone knew that parliament was called and everyone rumoured that it was intended to get the king what he wanted; one cannot fairly read into these vague phrases a foreknowledge of the parliamentary history of the next seven years. . . . That there was talk in government circles of settling the divorce without the pope — even loose talk of "provincial" independence — is not surprising and is vouched for by another French envoy, De Vaux, who reported in April 1530 that Henry spoke of dealing with the matter in his realm by the advice of his council and parliament without recourse to Rome. But it was only talk, even to the king himself. When he tried, several months later, to find means of turning words into deeds, he was told by a committee of canon and common lawyers, which had investigated the question, that parliament could in no way circumvent the pope and order the divorce to be decided by Canterbury. As Chapuys added, Henry was continuously threatening the pope with the power of parliament; yet there was so little genuine understanding or purpose in the threats that the solution later adopted without question was in 1530 ruled out as quite impossible. One cannot ask for better proof that in 1530 the government had not yet arrived at the policy of the break with Rome; the vigorous language of the disappointed king and his ministers was backed by no design or practical project. It is fair to say that no one can be shown to have prophesied in 1529, or even in 1530, the complete separation of England from the papacy, though many expected attacks on specific forms of papal authority. . . . After all, England, having been the most papalist and pope-ridden of countries in the fifteenth and early sixteenth centuries, had some way to go to attain the relative independence of France or even Spain. Henry's continued stand against Lutheran heresy made plain that he was not following the German example, and no one as yet — including Henry — could visualize a Catholic country without the pope.

What matters are not the words of observers but the deeds and intentions of Henry's government. Wolsey's failure to free Henry from Catherine of Aragon by means of the legatine court at Blackfriars was followed by the revocation of the case to Rome (July 1529), and for the three years after that everything turned on the issue whether Henry could be compelled to attend a trial at Rome or persuade the people to let the case be decided in England. All the manoeuvres on the king's part revolved around this central point. His intention was clear throughout: he wished to impress on Clement VII how much more comfortable it would be if he complied with the king's wishes. As a first step he called parliament. Left to themselves, the commons could be trusted to attack the church; they had shown their temper in 1515 and had been restive in 1523. The anti-clericalism of that first session was neither king-imposed nor king-inspired; at most it was permitted by the king. The commons' spontaneous action put pressure on the church and supplied Henry with ammunition for his attack at Rome — at Rome but not on Rome, for it is patent that Henry thought a divorce not sanctioned by

the papacy insufficient to secure a legitimate succession. The real purpose of parliament was to overawe the church; it is too readily forgotten that Henry could no more afford opposition among his own clergy if the pope permitted them to try the case in England than if he acted (as ultimately he did act) entirely without the pope. Attacks on the independence of the English church were not synonymous with attacks on Rome: hitherto king and pope had more commonly joined hands against the liberties of the English church.

To start with, therefore, Henry's policy was to bring the clergy to heel in anticipation of their being called upon to adjudicate in the divorce, and to put pressure on Clement to permit them to do so. It continued in 1530. Parliament stood adjourned and rumours abounded. The general threats which were reported back to France and Venice have already been noticed: in words Henry was certainly growing fiercer. In October 1530, repeating that by the customs of the realm an Englishman could not be compelled to stand trial outside England, he warned the pope that his continued refusal would raise the whole question of his authority; what right had he so to treat a prince of such dignity *"ut superiorem in terris non agnoscamus"*?[3] Lest we think that Henry had at last found a way out of his difficulties, let us remember that he had claimed to have no superior on earth as early as 1515, six years before he committed himself to exceedingly high views on papal authority in the *Assertio Septem Sacramentorum.* He was ready to make resounding claims, but he had no idea how to give effect to them. His only action, a proclamation forbidding the procuration of papal bulls designed to interfere with the reforming legislation of 1529, attacked the authority of papal legates only and not that of the Roman Curia at all; it did not touch the divorce in the very least. Despite all his brave words, Henry could do no more than spend a profitless year pursuing Cranmer's

[3] "That he recognized no superior on Earth."

donnish suggestion by collecting the opinions of the universities on the two points at issue — the rights of the divorce suit and the plea that Englishmen were privileged to have their cases tried in England — in the hope that the weight of authoritative pronouncements would change the pope's mind. When it did not, Henry contented himself with a vigorous protest and an appeal to general councils and unnamed English laws; there is no particle of a threat of schism. . . .

Some four years had passed since Henry first determined to exchange Catherine for Anne, but there was still no sign that anything had occurred to him except the hopeless plan of forcing the pope to agree to a trial in England which Catherine and her Spanish supporters refused to contemplate. One thing 1531 did produce — the surrender of the clergy to the threat of *praemunire* and their recognition of Henry as "their singular protector, only and supreme lord, and as far as the law of Christ allows also supreme head." Unable to make Rome do his will, the king at least succeeded in his other ambition of bringing the English clergy firmly under his control. Contrary to the accepted view, this title of 1531 looked back to the earlier vague claim that the kings of England had no superior on earth, rather than forward to the precise and effective position of jurisdictional and political authority which the same title was to imply in 1534. . . . The reservation which Fisher and Warham had inserted made nonsense of any claims more extreme than those which the English monarchy had steadily asserted over the church for centuries.[4] Certainly the words "as far as the law of Christ allows" were not meaningless; Henry himself interpreted them as excluding all spiritual authority and with it the one thing that mattered to him, the divorce. Replying to Tunstall's protest against the title, the king wrote that the

words *supremum caput* ought to be qualified by the addition of *in temporalibus*.[5] That the king is the temporal head of spiritual persons in his realm, he continued, appears from history: in the temporal sphere of

the persons of priests, their laws, their acts, and order of living . . . we . . . be indeed in this realm "Caput"; and because there is no man above us here, be indeed "Supremum Caput."

It may seem, and probably is, a disingenuous defence, but it is clear on one point: the king's title does not expressly deny the pope's spiritual headship or justify the withdrawal of England from the papal jurisdiction. As yet there is no policy of a "break with Rome.". . .

All this time Henry continued his policy of convincing the pope of the justice of his case, showing so little decision that hostile observers repeatedly concluded that he would give in, put Anne away, and return to Catherine. Reginald Pole heard similar reports: he alleged that Cromwell's advice rescued Henry from a fit of depression induced by his inability to see any way out. The king was bankrupt in ideas. He knew what he wanted; that neither he nor his ministers knew how to obtain it is proved by those years of bootless negotiations. Strong words having failed, he was less violent in language in 1531 than in 1530. In July he again suggested that Canterbury might be allowed to adjudicate; so far from wishing to withdraw from the Roman obedience, he still hoped to get papal approval for a trial in England. New envoys were despatched, only to report the obvious fact that nothing could be hoped for from Rome. By December 1531 Henry was so far reduced that he was ready to have the case tried in France, a safe enough compromise no doubt, but an astonishing surrender of his claims as a sovereign prince and greatly

---

[4] Fisher of Rochester and Warham of Canterbury had inserted the "insofar as the law of Christ" wording in the clause establishing Henry's title as "supreme head" of the Church.

[5] That is, that the "supreme head" was qualified by the understanding of this headship as extending only to temporal aspects of ecclesiastic affairs and persons.

at variance with the high language of 1530. The letter ended in threats so vague as to lack all import: if the king knew what he meant he carefully hid his knowledge. Early in 1532, when the pope seemed at last about to pronounce, Henry was desperate to have the case deferred; throughout 1531 and 1532 there run like a thread the silly machinations designed to bribe some cardinals to Henry's side and so prevent a decision in consistory. As late as this Henry was so firmly stuck in the mental processes of the past that he hoped to obtain his ends by the bestowal of English sees on Italians. Small wonder that early in 1532 Norfolk and Gardiner allegedly counselled the king to give up: it was about the only piece of advice they had left.

By this time, however, Norfolk and Gardiner were no longer the leading advisers, and diplomatic pressure at Rome was no longer the only policy. Late in 1531 Cromwell was at last admitted to that inner circle of councillors who really advised the king and governed the realm. Possibly the use of the term "empire" by Norfolk in conversation with Chapuys in January 1531 reflects the beginning of Cromwell's real influence; it can be shown — though not here — that it was he who introduced the notion of empire (= sovereignty) into the controversy. There are signs from that time onwards that the doomed policy of forcing Rome to act as England wished her to was being accompanied by steps of another kind. The clergy's surrender to the *praemunire* charge gave the king some positive gains, in particular the subsidies voted in an effort to propitiate the royal wrath; this was more than had resulted from all the energy spent in beating at the gates of Rome. However, the king's ultimate aims remained as unrealizable as before. If a new policy is to be discerned in the imposition of the title of supreme head, it is also clear that it was a policy pursued but halfheartedly and without a true understanding of where it might lead. In 1532 the undercurrent usurped the lead. At last parliament was turned against the pope. However harshly the sessions of 1529 and 1531 had dealt with the English clergy, they had not touched the papacy. But in 1532 parliament passed the first act of annates by which an important source of papal revenues was cut off and promoted the "Supplication against the Ordinaries"[6] which enabled Henry to follow up his nominal triumph of 1531 with a real triumph over the English clergy by forcing it to accept his control of ecclesiastical legislation. Since — as Maitland has taught us — the English church had no legislative independence in the later middle ages, this meant that its dependence was transferred from pope to king; the manoeuvre based on the Supplication — the "Submission of the Clergy" — was a real though a masked attack on the pope's authority in England.

Thus 1532 saw the inauguration of the policy which was to culminate in the complete destruction of the Roman jurisdiction in England and England's complete withdrawal from the Roman obedience. It also saw the first use for that purpose of the instrument by means of which the revolution was to be accomplished, a point of great significance which can only be hinted at here: there is good reason for supposing that Cromwell, who deliberately made a career in parliament, introduced the king to the potentialities of statute. In the sudden eruption of a new policy, Cromwell's hand is manifest. It was he who brought the Supplication — first started by the commons in 1529 but then not driven home — to the attention of the government, who prepared the final draft, and who managed the manoeuvre involved in its employment. He drafted the famous clause in the first act of annates which postponed its effect until the king should have tried further negotiations with Rome. In itself that clause marked a defeat for the new policy; it may be conjectured, on the basis of the developments already described, that Cromwell's

[6] That was the heading of the detailed parliamentary complaints against the higher clergy and church government of laymen; Elton's point is that the "Supplication" led to the "Submission."

act proved as yet too drastic for Henry, so that his first anti-papal measure had to be adapted to the purposes of that other policy which had relied for some three years on finding means to coerce the pope into compliance.

Like all its predecessors, this means also failed: Clement was not to be persuaded by the distant power of England while the neighbouring power of the emperor remained hostile. And so, a year later, in the session of February-April 1533, the act in restraint of appeals to Rome, with its great proclamation of national sovereignty, signalled the triumph of the radical policy — the break with Rome. The prehistory of this act provides the last proof of the two separate policies which have been traced in this paper, and of the fact that Cromwell sponsored the one that proved successful. There survive two drafts for acts of parliament in the hands of Sir Thomas Audley, who had succeeded More as keeper of the great seal in May 1532, which indicate that even late in 1532 some doubt remained as to the best way of getting the divorce legalized in the realm. One of them would have given parliamentary endorsement to a divorce pronounced by the archbishop of Canterbury; this represented only an *ex post facto* sanction and not a parliamentary policy. The other intended to give to the archbishops parliamentary authority to act in the divorce in the pope's place; it is the climax of that policy which had persistently endeavoured to get Rome to remit the case to England — the culmination of all those complaints, recitals of privileges, and vague threats of hostile action in which Henry had indulged ever since Wolsey's failure in the summer of 1529. It used parliament, but only to permit Canterbury for once to stand in Rome's stead: not based on any profound principle, it was the half-hearted sort of thing that the lawyers' decision had held up in 1530. Its preamble recites the divine law against a man marrying his brother's wife, laments the long delays, and accuses the pope of aspiring to usurp the rights of princes; it is throughout full of apologies, self-justification, and polite references to "the popes holynes."

The statute actually passed, on the other hand, not only provided for a general prohibition of appeals to Rome — that is, it dealt with a wide issue of general significance instead of confining itself to the particular matter of the divorce — but also included a preamble which described in unequivocal language a theory of England as a sovereign state in which no other potentate might interfere. That it was Cromwell who evolved this measure, and how he overcame some remaining fears and doubts which proclaimed themselves in apologetic and justificatory phrases, has been described elsewhere. Right to the end of the long-drawn conflict the two policies — one pursued since 1529, the other introduced by Cromwell in 1532 — vied with each other for the king's approval. So reluctant was Henry to take the decisive step that even towards the end of 1532 he could still toy with a partial measure designed to keep the door open at least an inch or two, even while a simple and thorough policy based on a devastating principle was offered to him. Cromwell's grandiose conceptions triumphed, but it seems to have been a near thing.

The Reformation, then, was not the inevitable development of the text-books. Whether it would have come anyway it is idle to speculate; but it came in the 1530's simply because Henry's desire for his divorce was baulked by an international situation which made co-operation with the papacy impossible, and it came as it did because Thomas Cromwell produced a plan which achieved Henry's ends by destroying the papal power and jurisdiction in England and by creating in England an independent sovereign state. This policy was not present from the start; it had to overcome much caution and conservatism as well as fear of the consequences before its bold simplicity was permitted to develop. The Henrician Reformation reflects the ideas — one may say, the political philosophy — of Thomas Cromwell.

WOLSEY: PRELUDE TO A REVOLUTION

PHILIP HUGHES

Father Philip Hughes was born in Manchester, England, in 1895. After prelimonary studies, he obtained his licentiate in science at Louvain in 1921. In his long and varied career he has taught and studied in England, Rome, and America and has been the recipient of numerous awards and honors, among them honorary degrees from Louvain, the National University of Ireland and Notre Dame (Indiana). Since 1955 he has held a professorship in history at Notre Dame, where he has pursued studies that have contained his interests in sixteenth-century history. In addition to his large-scale *History of the Church to 1517* (3 volumes), Father Hughes is also the author of a study of John Lingard's historical method, another on the Church in the seventeenth century, and—his most important book—*The Reformation in England* (3 volumes).

CARDINAL WOLSEY'S fall from power in the autumn of 1529 is one of those spectacular events that really are as great as they seem to be. Never, in all English history, has there been a subject so plentifully endowed with authority and so powerful in the use of it, so wealthy, so magnificent; and never has any man stirred up in his career such a general, variously assorted, tide of bitter, determined hatred. The cardinal is not indeed an actor in the great affair of the change of religion: barely a year after his fall death removed him from the scene. But the guns were already loaded and trained that were to deliver the first broadside against the papal supremacy; it was only a bare seven weeks after Wolsey died that they were fired. Such had been his career that the cardinal may be said to have created, in almost all its parts, the king's opportunity, the critical situation of the two years that followed his own death, the crisis from which the religion of the English emerged a royal and no longer a papal thing, national and no longer Catholic. Wolsey's fall was truly "the prelude to a revolution," and it was all but necessarily so.

What had Wolsey been in the long years of his power? The simplest thing is to say, tritely, that he had been everything. As Lord Chancellor he was the principal minister of state for the government of the country. From his seat in the court of Chancery, with the needed strong hand, he controlled the endless conflict of legal systems which was now a permanent menace to good government, and from this point of view he was "the chancellor *par excellence.*" His work here is his greatest title to fame. He was no less diligent and masterful in that "courte at Westminster commonly called the Starre chamber"; so diligent, indeed, that he has a claim to be considered the first creator of its fame. With Wolsey in control, this court became the centre to which flowed in all complaints of oppression by the mighty, of neglect and delay of justice, of insubordination to the royal will in administration. The cardinal was prompt, he was just, and extremely vigorous; and he never hesitated to call into his court for settlement cases he thought would be better settled there than in other courts. And so he came to stir up the most fatal animosity of all, the hatred of the lawyers and

Reprinted with permission of The Macmillan Company and of Burns and Oates, Ltd. from *The Reformation in England* by Philip Hughes (1953), I, pp. 109–15.

judges of the courts of Common Law.[1]

Of Parliament Wolsey made almost no use at all; it met only once in the fourteen years of his power. The same dictatorial temperament drove him also to dispense, as far as this was possible, with the council itself.

The cardinal also controlled, wholly, and personally, the country's foreign affairs; and here, in more than one way, he fell foul, first of the financial and commercial interests and, ultimately, of every man who had an acre of land to be taxed or a house or a cow or a pig. For his foreign policy involved wars costly beyond anything England had ever known; and it ended in disaster, with all the bills unpaid. After the long twenty-four years' peace of the cautious Henry VII this was indeed a change; and Wolsey was the man responsible for the change. There was the war against France in 1511–1514, and the emperor's expedition of 1515–1516 against France which England subsidised, and the war against France of 1521–1525 and then, what very largely broke the cardinal, the war against the emperor — with France, this time, as ally — in 1528–1529. Henry VII had left behind him a huge treasure, but long before the debacle of 1529 this had all been spent. In 1511, the last year of the old peace régime, the national expenses were £64,000. In the first year of the first war (1512) they rose to £270,000 and in the next to £700,000. The Parliament of 1513–1514 was asked to vote unheard of taxes — a shilling in the pound on all incomes and a capital levy, at the same rate, on all property and goods. In 1515 the cardinal descended on the war profiteers, and also began an extensive resumption of lands granted by the crown. When the war of 1521 began, the king had no money left. The London merchants were persuaded to lend £20,000 and another £350,000 was obtained by forced loans from nobles, clergy,

gentry, and all who might be thought to have money to lend. Then, in 1525, Wolsey appeared in the House of Commons to ask for £800,000 — twelve and a half times the total expenses fourteen years earlier — the money to be obtained by a tax of four shillings in the pound on land and movable property; while from the clergy he demanded half a year's income, to be paid in five annual instalments. As the forced loan of the previous year was still in process of collection, the wild and universal hatred that now began to rise may be imagined.

To make matters worse, the war, this time, went badly. Wolsey had had hopes, in 1523, of being elected pope and had staked much on his success. But in the conclave his name was no more than mentioned. The emperor, Charles V, England's ally, whom the cardinal thought he had in his pocket, double crossed him with ease for the second time. Wolsey, in order to finance the war, had now, in 1525, to approach the king for money from the king's own funds. England had no choice but to retire from the field, and did so, unluckily, on the eve of her imperial ally's greatest victory over France, the famous battle of Pavia (February 24, 1525). We had lost in the war, where our ally had won all, our money was at an end, and now we would have no say in the peace. This was indeed ruinous for a statesman's credit, and Wolsey made a bold effort to gather in money yet once again and to renew the war. And so there was a second forced loan — wholly unauthorized this time, for Parliament was not summoned — called the "amicable grant." It was a capital levy of one-sixth of the laity's goods as well as one-sixth of their incomes, with double that amount from the clergy.

But now, the summer of 1525, there were riots all over the wealthy southeastern counties and in East Anglia too. The clergy, above all, were bitterly hostile. For the first time in his life the cardinal had to retreat, and it was a crowning disaster that he now made peace with France in such a way that, simultaneously, he made an enemy for life of the emperor.

[1] Because every extension of jurisdiction of an equitable sort, so attractive to subjects with long memories of the failure of justice in the fifteenth century, cut into the practice and profit of the common law advocates and judges.

Wolsey, by this time, had lost all sense of the realities of the situation. Never in her history had England enjoyed anything like a parity of resources with either of the powers locked already in the fight that was to last for yet another thirty years. Whichever of them we chose to support, the Empire or France, they were allies we could neither trust nor control; and now we could not even bribe or fee them. Of the two it was the emperor whose enmity could harm England the more, for he was the sovereign of those Low Countries trade with which was the principal source of English prosperity.[2] Wolsey's declaration of war on Charles V in 1528 was, then, the greatest of all his follies. Six months before this the emperor's ambassador had written from London that "The whole country is roused against the cardinal . . . he is universally hated"; and it was the envoy of the new French ally who said, in respect of the new policy, "Wolsey is playing a terrible game, for I believe he is the only Englishman who wants a war with Flanders." As in 1525 there were, once more, riots all over the south-east, and presently an arrangement was made with Charles that trade with the Low Countries should continue despite the war.

As yet — the spring of 1528 — the difficulties of Henry VIII's marriage suit had barely begun to show themselves in their real insuperability, but Wolsey, for the second time in five years, was already facing the country with a record of disgrace and disaster in a war that no one had wanted but himself. Only the king stood between him and a fearful end. Another short twelve months and the fiasco of the cardinal's contrivances in the marriage suit would lose him his one protector.

It remains to consider another element in Wolsey's well merited unpopularity at the moment when that last misfortune befell him, and to consider it as having the closest connection with the disastrous foreign policy and its ruinous finance. That element is Wolsey's position, during the greater part of all this time, as the permanent resident legate of the pope, a kind of vice-pope, indeed, for England. For the effect of this office, or rather of the way in which it was exercised, not only alienated the clergy, and especially the bishops, from Wolsey and, perhaps, from the Holy See, but it linked with the cause of the Holy See all the misery and humiliation that maddened the laymen; and it fanned the habitual anti-clericalism of many of them into something very like fury.

Wolsey had begged for appointment as resident legate *a latere*[3] almost from the moment he was created cardinal. What he desired was an authority over the whole of English ecclesiastical life as complete as that which he exercised over the nation as the king's chief minister; and in the end he received it, little by little, more and more amply, according as the needs of the pope's foreign policy grew more acute. The first commission, dated May 17, 1518, makes Wolsey the colleague of Cardinal Lorenzo Campeggio, Leo X's legate to the "peace conference" about to meet in London: it was extorted as the price of the Italian legate's admission into the realm. A few months later the two legates were given wide powers to reform monasteries, and Wolsey was allowed to retain these after Campeggio's departure in 1519. In 1521 these powers were renewed for another two years and additional powers granted. In 1523 the next pope, Adrian VI, maintaining his predecessor's refusal to extend the powers for Wolsey's lifetime, renewed them nevertheless for another five years; and in 1524 Clement VII made the long coveted grant for life, and still further extended the legate's powers, begging Wolsey, however, to handle the friars gently, so much did the pope dread the clamour that would otherwise ensue.

The whole local, supplementary law and

2 As the center of the English wool trade.

3 *Legatus a latere* was in effect the title of one exercising full papal authority in a country in his own person, as opposed to the *legatus natus*, who had a much more limited power, to be exercised usually in the country of his birth (*a latere*: from the side, i.e., sent from the Pope's side with full powers).

practice of the *ecclesia anglicana*[4] was now placed at Wolsey's mercy. He proceeded to suppress, by way of reformation, and to the profit of the colleges he was planning at Oxford and Ipswich, some twenty-one religious houses, and the Church in Ireland (also made subject to him) he proposed to transform complete, by reducing the number of archbishops from four to two and the bishops' sees from thirty to ten. To this end he procured the appointment of Dr. John Allen — a clerical rascal of a type Wolsey kept by him for the less reputable part of his work — to be Archbishop of Dublin and Lord Chancellor of Ireland.

As legate Wolsey gradually drew into his own hands whatever ecclesiastical business brought with it any money profit. He interfered extensively in the elections of abbots; he deposed them; and he was not above taking presents from the interested parties. He sent his officers to make visitations of the various dioceses and encouraged them to lecture the negligent absentee prelates — he who, in all his episcopal life, never so much as saw any one of the cathedrals of the five sees he occupied! In despite of long custom he revived the old papal practice of presenting to livings[5] wherever he chose, without in any way consulting the wishes of the bishops — thus bringing himself under the operation of the Statutes of Provisors and Praemunire. And, the most tremendous interference of all, he began to take over from the bishops their diocesan administration, sometimes working through his own commissaries and sometimes allowing the bishops to continue to rule, but as his delegates — for a share of the fees. He even did this with the Archbishop of Canterbury, who found himself forbidden to act through his famous courts of Arches and of Audience, and his provincial jurisdiction reduced to nothing, "a shadow and an image of an archbishop and legate," the old man complained, "void of authority and jurisdiction."[6] The legate also seized — what

he had no right at all to seize, since this was a matter of English law and not of Canon law — the archbishop's vast jurisdiction over probate; and out of this he proceeded to make a fortune by charging immense fees to the executors who appeared before him.[7] And when Warham began to fight the matter Wolsey threatened to inveigle him in a praemunire. Wolsey the legate must ignore praemunire, and resist it as a most noxious affront to the Church's sovereign status; but Wolsey the Lord Chancellor could find praemunire an excellent weapon to compel obedience to himself as legate.

It is little wonder that the legate, when his own hour struck, preferred to face even the Common Law judges of the King's Bench[8] rather than answer to his peers in Parliament. There, said the French Ambassador, himself a bishop, the bishops "had already chosen judges after their liking," lay lords, to wit, long envious of the cardinal's career, embittered by the immense losses in which his policies had involved the country, and by the close connection between those policies and the "legacy."

Wolsey had, in fact, been always a great churchman, in the worst sense of the word — in the sense that the church system was for him the supreme vested interest. This is not to describe him as a man who lacked faith. Wolsey believed, undoubtedly, and prayed too, at times, like the most of us. But the ecclesiastical system was his living and his career, and it was a time when, as has been said, to far too many well-placed clerics the papacy itself chiefly appealed as the greatest benefice of all. In this interest of Wolsey in the papacy, it has been well argued, lies the unifying thread of his vast and complicated public career. His first recorded letter, written when he had scarcely emerged from obscurity as a clever industrious administrator in the royal household, speaks of Rome as the source whence ought to come — not to Wolsey only, but to the

[4] "The Church in England."
[5] The filling of vacant church benefices is the act of "presentment."
[6] The "old man" in question was William Warham.

[7] The "proving" (probate) of wills and testaments, as it involved a sacred oath, was a church matter handled in ecclesiastical courts.
[8] A common law court exercising jurisdiction in what we should call criminal cases.

king — "honour and all the furtherance of his affairs in time to come." Four years later Wolsey is Archbishop of York and in full charge, and the Venetian Ambassador is told that "the pope is now so linked with the king that words cannot exaggerate their mutual goodwill; so that, in the affairs of France, the policy of England will be that of Rome." And not in "the affairs of France" alone.

For the next fifteen years (1514–1529) that statement was to be verified by the event, time after time. *Ubi Petrus ibi Anglia*;[9] and the great central point of the national diplomacy and war was the preservation of the temporal independence of the Holy See menaced, now by France, and now by Spain. It was unfortunate in the extreme that this first incursion on the grand scale into the whirlpools of international diplomacy, on the part of an Englishman of genius, should be made while as yet English resources were far from adequate to what the occasion called for; and it was no less unfortunate that the Holy See was occupied during all these years by the two most vacillating — not to say tergiversating — the two least reliable, and least competent, of all the popes who have had to play the diplomatic game. But through it all, Wolsey remained faithful to his principle — and to his hope (a thing of later growth with him) that one day he would himself be pope.

"Every change in [Wolsey's] attitude towards other European powers coincided with a change in the policy of the papal curia. So long as Wolsey influenced England's conduct, Henry VIII remained the favourite son of the Roman Church." It was the call of Pope Julius II in 1511 which brought Henry into his first war — the defence of the pope against Louis XII of France threatening schism; when, in 1514, England made peace with Louis this was because the new pope, Leo X, was making peace with him and asked Henry to do the same; a year later, when the same pope made his peace with the new king of France, Francis I, after the unhappy gaffe that put the pope on the wrong side at Marignano,[10] England again made peace; in 1521 France was again at war with the pope, and England had joined with the emperor as the pope's ally. England did not, in 1526, join the pope and France in the war of the League of Cognac (against Charles) because England was all but bankrupt. But England came into the war two years later. Once England broke with the pope there was no more continental war so long as Henry VIII lived, another sixteen years — save the expedition of 1544–1545 to Boulogne.

The "legacy" and the foreign policy were closely connected. It was not strange, seeing that the foreign minister was the legate himself. Nor is it strange that disaster to the country through the legate's mismanagement of foreign affairs should spell disaster to much more than the legate's own career; " . . . the friendship with which I have inspired the king towards his holiness," so the legate wrote at the end of 1527, "will be permanent, unless some occasion should be offered for alienating the king's mind, in which event it will never be in my power to serve his holiness." That "occasion" was by now already offered: the divorce suit, in the terrible inevitable way of such things, had begun to gather speed. Soon it would be thundering down the ways with a clatter to confound wise men everywhere and the good. Eighteen months after that letter to Rome, Wolsey, trying at Blackfriars, with Campeggio as his colleague, the king's petition, and knowing now beyond all doubt how this must go to Rome and how it must end, writes a pendant to the letter of 1527. The pope, he says, "has refused all the concessions which, relying on him, I had promised the king . . . and that will be my ruin."

[9] Elliptical for "where Peter [Rome] is, there also England stands."

[10] The Battle of Marignano, September 13 and 14, 1515, saw the French under Francis I defeat the great Swiss mercenaries of the Empire. Leo X made his peace with Francis at Bologna.

THE FATE OF THE MONASTERIES

DAVID KNOWLES

Born Michael Clive Knowles in 1896 in Warwickshire, England, but in scholarship known by his religious name, Dom David Knowles, O.S.B., is one of the greatest living historians. Ordained a priest in 1922, after a period of study at Christ's College, Cambridge, Dom David began the literary and academic career which has brought him numerous honors. Regius Professor of Modern History in Cambridge from 1954 to 1963, he has also been the president of the Royal Historical Society; Ford's lecturer in English history, Oxford; British Academy Raleigh lecturer; Creighton lecturer, London; and the recipient of fellowships and honorary degrees. His fame rests on *The Monastic Order in England, The Religious Houses of Medieval England*, and his three-volume *The Religious Orders in England*, as well as on his *The English Mystical Tradition, The Evolution of Medieval Thought, The Historian and Character*, and other books and articles too numerous to mention.

AT THE CONCLUSION of a work that has presented the history of the monastic order and of the religious orders in England from the revival of the tenth century to the dissolution of the monasteries almost exactly six centuries later, it is natural to look back upon the path that has been traversed, as climbers might look back upon the silhouette of an *arête*.[1]

Before doing so, we should do well to remind ourselves that the monastic way of life, to which all the medieval religious orders were assimilated in greater or less degree, had been in existence for more than six centuries before the age of Dunstan,[2] and continued to flourish in Catholic countries during and after the age of the Reformation. Indeed, in the previous chapter we have seen how the last spark of the old fire remained in this country to be merged in the new flame. The monasticism of the counter-Reformation had in its turn an

eclipse in the age of enlightenment and revolution; it witnessed a third spring in the nineteenth century and still flourishes; indeed, it has expanded yearly even while these volumes have been in the writing.

Yet for all this, the assumption of English antiquarians and historians in the past, that monasticism was something medieval, and had passed "like the baseless fabric of a vision" with the medieval world, had in it a part, at least, of the truth. Monasticism as an integral part of society, and as an economic and cultural factor of the first importance, was a specific element in the medieval world between the decline of the Roman empire and the Reformation: as such it passed wherever and whenever the medieval framework disappeared, and it is hard to see how it could ever again come to take such a place in society, save perhaps in a comparable state of utter disruption and depopulation following upon the collapse of a world civilization of which Christianity was the only surviving element. Much of what has been written in the past of medieval monasticism has in-

---

[1] A mountain ridge or spine-like projection.
[2] Saint Dunstan (924–88), Archbishop of Canterbury and proponent in England of Benedictine reform movements.

From David Knowles, *The Religious Orders in England* (Cambridge, England, 1961), III, pp. 456–68. Reprinted by permission of Cambridge University Press, New York and London.

deed been vitiated by a failure to realize that it had within it elements that were temporary together with those that were permanent, and while Catholic and romantic writers have confused social, cultural or institutional features of medieval monasticism with the religious life in itself, Protestant and secularist historians have often treated the permanent, essential elements as if they were as perishable as the medieval garments in which they were clothed. Only if this distinction is borne in mind can it be seen how the purely religious and spiritual institute, such as was conceived by a Cassian, a Benedict, a Columba, or a Bede, was caught up into the very fabric of a continental society, of which it became and remained for many centuries a wealthy, powerful and even a dominant part.

When Dunstan and his companions initiated a great revival in England, society throughout western Europe was in need of, and docile to, spiritual and intellectual leadership. Monks, and monks principally and often monks alone, were the repositories of religious doctrine and educational opportunities; in consequence, they multiplied exceedingly, and rapidly attained an economic as well as a religious and cultural supremacy, and it was natural and inevitable that society outside the walls of a monastery should look to it for its spiritual leaders and receive from them an imprint of their own qualities. During the eleventh and the greater part of the twelfth centuries monasticism reached its peak of influence and dynamic force at Cluny and Cîteaux, and its light was focused upon Christendom by a Lanfranc and a Bernard, by a Gregory VII and a Eugenius III. If it was something of a rhetorical exaggeration to say, as contemporaries said, that the world had become one great Cîteaux, it was but the bare truth to say that the whole Western Church had received such an infusion of the monastic spirit as to colour its whole spiritual and devotional life.

The material result of this was seen in the numberless religious foundations, in the vast and ever-increasing army of monks and conversi,[3] in the great buildings that began to dominate the landscape and the rich estates controlled by the monks. From being in the early eleventh century primarily a religious and an educational force, they became towards its end, both by force of numbers, by virtue of their appeal to all classes, and by sheer economic weight as landlords (and somewhat later as producers) an immense social power. It should perhaps be added, that the character and outlook of the older monastic and canonical orders deprived their power of any political force, even within the sphere of ecclesiastical policy. The medieval monks never became, as did the Byzantine monks on occasion, and religious orders in later times, a "pressure group" or a party within the Church.

The "Benedictine centuries" are generally thought to have ended with the death of St. Bernard in 1153. Thenceforward, while on the one hand the monarchies of France and England were consolidating their power and developing their judicial and financial control of their people, while the Church, centred upon the papacy, was perfecting a legal and financial system, and an extensive bureaucracy of its own, the intellectual life of Europe was shifting from the monasteries to the cathedral schools and the young universities. Concurrently, the growth of population, the increase of trade, and the expansion of all forms of agrarian exploitation were lessening the relative importance of the monasteries in almost every region. For a time, indeed, the tendencies of the age were masked by the emergence and wide diffusion of the friars, who seemed to contemporaries (what indeed they set out in part to be) the ultimate issue of the monastic spirit, the communication of the religious life to the last groups hitherto untouched by it, the urban populations and the poor throughout the land. In fact, however, the friars dealt a heavy blow to monastic prestige, at first by outbidding the monks in fervour, then by draining many

3 Converts.

of the reservoirs of talent and virtue that would otherwise have served the older orders, next by giving an entirely new challenge to the monks by their intellectual celebrity, and finally by attracting so many recruits, good, bad and indifferent that the edge of their ideal was blunted, and in course of time, both by their direct opposition to the monks and by the criticisms which they themselves incurred, they became the weakest and most vulnerable corps in the army of the religious. All orders, in fact, had in the days of expansion gone beyond the frontiers that could be permanently held. Already in the late thirteenth century the numbers of monks and canons were slowly diminishing; those of the friars reached their peak about 1300, when both the number of religious establishments in the country and the population within them touched a high-water mark which was never again to be attained or even approached.

Indeed, from about the middle of the thirteenth century the old orders of monks and canons were losing their commanding position in medieval society. They had ceased for some time both to be a dynamic, formative element, and to be regarded as the upholders of Christendom by their prayers and penances; they had hardened into what was merely a constituent part of the national life, half religious, half economic, alongside of the landowners, great and small, and the growing craft and commercial interests of the towns. In a society still conventionally, and in part actually, dominated by religious modes of thought they were regarded as an essential part of the body politic, just as the friars were still indispensable in the schools and pulpits, and if their social function of intercession was no longer reckoned important, individuals still hoped to benefit by their prayers and Masses, nor were they as yet (1350) seriously regarded as unprofitable proprietors of desirable lands. Towards the end of the fourteenth century, in fact, they attained within their walls an architectural and material splendour greater than ever

before, and in the artificial society and new-won wealth of the decades of war with France and domestic intrigues among the great families they, or at least the greater ones among them, were a kind of extension of the contemporary world of chivalry.

Thereafter, when that world faded and was succeeded by a world in which money and property meant everything, and in which deep intellectual or spiritual interests were wanting, a world which was shortly to be shaken by the impact of new doctrines and new ideals, the monasteries and religious orders in general receded more and more from the forefront of society. Though those who uttered their criticisms of the monks were perhaps neither many nor influential, there was a new feeling of resentment abroad. The monks were accused of sloth, and of being the drones of the community; those who leased or managed their lands were land-hungry, and the slow but significant growth of population and mercantile wealth put a new pressure upon the land market. Though there was little increase in the aggregate wealth of the religious and little change in the use they made of it or in their own habit of life, a feeling was abroad that great revenues were being used selfishly or aimlessly. Few of those who felt thus had any programme for a better distribution or use of wealth, and in the event the transference of property at the Dissolution did not to any significant extent benefit other religious, educational or charitable institutes, or assist impoverished classes; no social injustice was in fact remedied or any national end served. Nevertheless, in the last decades before the end the new generation of gentry and government servants lacked altogether the conservative reverence towards the Church that had prevailed a century earlier. As for the friars, though they held no property of any value and were probably living on a bare subsistence income from charity past and present, they also were accused of draining the country's wealth.

While the social and economic position of the religious was thus changing and ultimately deteriorating, the energy and spirit within the Orders were following something of the same curve. In the two centuries that followed the revival under Dunstan the monks had an ideal and a message which both they and those around them could see and appreciate. The monastic and the canonical life was a clearly defined, severely disciplined one of prayer and work, sufficiently austere to inspire respect in those outside and to produce the fruits of the gospel promises in those who followed it with perseverance. The careful reader of the *Regularis Concordia*,[4] of Lanfranc's monastic constitutions and of the early Cistercian constitutions cannot fail to perceive that these documents were composed to be followed, and that a life based upon them would have been not unworthy of the ideals of the gospel; it would have been a life only comprehensible or defensible on the supposition of the truth of the Christian revelation, a life in which natural human satisfactions, interests and activities were abandoned by those who believed that they had here no lasting city, but sought one to come. This high endeavour was reiterated and emphasized by the manifestos of the new Orders of the twelfth century, and again by the early friars of the thirteenth, and despite the failures, the scandals, and the criticisms of the age it is probable that even as late as the middle of the thirteenth century the religious life in all its forms was normally maintained in its essentials at most of the larger conventual houses. In the fourteenth century, however, changes were made in the tenor and structure of the life which materially affected its character. The frequentation of the universities, the increased part taken by a greater number of officials in administering the estates and funds, the mitigation of

the Rule in the matter of meat-eating, the introduction of periods of relaxation and excursion, of holidays and of pocket-money, seriously altered the rhythm of life for the majority of the adult community. Further changes, unauthorized by any legislation, but arising when the bonds of discipline were loosed by the Great Schism, gave numerous individuals exceptions and privileges of all kinds which lowered still further what may be called the normal spiritual temperature of the house. While it was no doubt still possible for an individual to live a strict and holy life, he could only do so by refusing in practice to take advantage of relaxations or to solicit any favours. Whereas the monk in private place of the early twelfth century would have needed to take deliberate action to escape the full regular life, the monk of the late fourteenth century would have needed equal determination to remain within its ambit. Finally, in the last fifty years before the end, though no further official mitigations of observance took place, an indefinable spiritual rusticity took hold of a majority of the houses; recruits expected and even demanded the normal amenities of the day — the wage-system, official privilege, regular times of holiday, and the rest. With the exception of the Carthusians, the Bridgettines and the Observant Franciscans, the religious life in England was humanly speaking easier and less spiritually stimulating in 1530 than it had been a century earlier.

What, we may ask, were the causes of this, and at what point in the long story did the religious orders miss their way, or at least begin to stray down the primrose path when a return to the ascent of the mountain was hard if not impossible? A general answer, and one true within very wide limits, would be that the religious throughout these centuries did but follow the general rhythm of Christendom. Not only upon the monks, but upon the higher and lower clergy and perhaps even upon the layfolk religious convention made less austere demands in 1530 than it had done

---

[4] The work of St. Dunstan's circle, *Regularis Concordia Angliae Nationis,* was written by the reform-minded Abbot of Glastonbury, Aethelwold, a Benedictine monk. Aethelwold's book was sponsored by King Edgar's *witan,* or council, and is chiefly important as a concordance of rules governing monastic life in England but based on European reform movements (ca. 970).

in 1100. The penal and penitential discipline, the precepts of fasting, the strictness of overhead control, the levels of comfort and wealth had all moved in the direction of mitigation, and there had been no compensatory developments of sacramental devotion, preaching, social works of charity or private methods of prayer such as become so common among all classes and all confessions in the latter part of the sixteenth century. When all allowances and reservations have been made, we must still say that the Church throughout Europe was at a lower level of discipline and observance, and exhibited more symptoms of mental and moral sickness than at any time since the Gregorian reform. Though England on the whole showed less alarming signs of decline than most of the continental countries it is certain that here, too, the faith and charity of many were cold and that, if a phrase used on an earlier page may be repeated, the Catholic religion was being reduced to its lowest terms. If this was true of the whole body ecclesiastic, it could not but be so with the religious orders, which were now nothing if not racy of the soil.

If, however, we insist on asking what were the contributory factors to this decline within the Orders themselves, and what their responsibility, the following considerations may be proposed.

There was, first, the great wealth of the religious and (what is another aspect of the same circumstance) the vast number of their houses. The wealth, indeed, they shared with all other ecclesiastical institutions, with bishoprics, benefices, chapters and the Curia itself. It had come to them in the first place unasked, and it had grown to vast dimensions partly by natural increase and economic development, and partly by prudent administration, but in the long run it had been a prime cause of spiritual weakness to the monasteries as to all the ministers and organs of the Church, great and small. It was not necessary for the proper functioning of the monastic life, and it was the parent of luxury, of strife and of worldliness. Yet it clung like pitch,

if only because no individual or group of individuals could in fact do anything to rid themselves of it. Nothing but a completely fresh start, or a social revolution, could have changed things. The numbers also had come unasked, and every age has taught anew the lesson which no institution has been willing to learn, that in the long run quality fluctuates in inverse relation to quantity. Even the wisest of saints have been unable to decide when the duty of preserving a precious heritage takes precedence over the duty of offering a spiritual treasure freely to all. In fact, saturation point had been reached in England even in the century of greatest fervour; there were not enough true vocations to go round; and the religious life became gradually and insensibly an occupation, an apprenticeship to a craft, rather than a "conversion" or a dedication to the service of God and the imitation of Christ.

In addition to these general sources of weakness, there were others that affected the black monks most, and others through sympathy or imitation. There was, first of all, what may be called the original sin of English black monk polity after the Conquest: the feudal ties of the heads of houses, of which a sequel, if not a result, was the immersion of the abbots in affairs external to their abbey, together with their gradual separation, physical, financial and psychological, from their monks, and their consequent inability to stand to their sons in the only true relationship, that of spiritual fatherhood and mutual love. Like the theological condition from which the metaphor has been taken, this situation was no fault of the individual, and it could be overcome to a greater or less degree, but never fully. The medieval abbot could not be among his monks as one that served. This defect passed also by kinship or inheritance to the other orders, such as the Cistercians, who were founded in free alms. There too, though less markedly, the abbot acquired a state apart from his monks, and it was the status of the black monk abbots which gave rise to the convenient legal fiction that the abbot was the proprietor of his abbey: a concept that weighed heavily in favour of a sitting abbot when disposition was mooted, that ensured for a quondam an establishment of his own, that in the final cataclysm gave a superior a pension often larger than that of all his subjects put together, and that allowed the legal chicanery by which the abbey of a treasonable superior was held to escheat to the Crown.

Of quite another kind was a weakness that was a misfortune rather than a fault. Throughout the Benedictine centuries the basic employment of the monks of the cloister had been the making and decorating of books. Once granted that agricultural and craft work was not for priests, this was an ideal employment. It was necessary for the continuance of the daily life, liturgical, spiritual, intellectual and administrative; it was in itself often either mentally or devotionally satisfying; by including all the processes of book manufacture and ornament it made use of various talents; it could be taken up and laid down again and again without hurt or loss; it furnished a literature for the whole of the educated class and in its finest forms it gave full scope for artistic talent of the very highest order. Moreover, it was an easy transition from the copying of literary masterpieces and biographies to pass to the imitation of their style and to original composition. But from the middle of the thirteenth century its unique position was assailed. Writing of all kinds was now a common attainment and a lucrative employment outside the monastery, and in the more settled and complex conditions of life scribes and artists, clerical and even secular, began to compete with and even to supplant the claustral writer and illuminator. Writing in the monastery became more utilitarian and for domestic ends, till in the late fifteenth century it was a fossilized and artificial occupation from which the sense of urgency and of achievement had disappeared. No substitute occurred to take its place; indeed, no perfect substitute has been found to this day. In the monasteries of the counter-Reformation teaching and works of theology and scholarship were pursued as the normal monastic employment, but nothing has been found to fit all types of ability, while these and all alternatives imply sooner or later frequent physical absence from the cloister and considerable distraction of life which tells against monastic recollection and solitude. One of the troubles in monasteries in the late fifteenth century was undoubtedly the absence of satisfactory and satisfying occupation.

Another disability came from the lack of a spiritual doctrine, an *ascèse*[5] to fit the changing world. In the simpler and more silent world of the Benedictine centuries a meditative reading of the Scriptures and the Fathers, and the liturgical prayer in choir were able almost alone to mould the character and spirit and lead it to recollection and prayer. The rise of the schools and the training in law and dialectic gradually increased all mental activity while at the same time life in the monastery itself became less remote and more distracted. A new spiritual approach was needed to supplement the training given by exercises in deportment, by the customs of the house, by Victorine doctrine, and by the memorizing of the psalter, but it was not forthcoming. The monks made little use either of the scholastic analysis of the acquired and infused virtues or of the later and fuller teaching of the mystics of Germany and Flanders or of the still later *devotio moderna*[6] of the Brethren of the Common Life. To the end they seem to have preserved a ghost of the method, or lack of method, of a simpler age, and in practice this implied the lack of any personal training or direction in the ascetic and spiritual life for the individual during the later Middle Ages. Not until the days of the great Spaniards, Franciscans, Carmelites and Jesuits, was the monastic world recalled to the cultivation by the individual of the life of prayer, and given the instruction fitted to a generation familiar with the

[5] "Asceticism."
[6] "The New Piety," the famous movement of educational and devotional reforms, ca. 1400–1500.

printed book and the formal method.

Yet if some of the ills of the religious were due to misfortune, they cannot escape all responsibility for others. Of these three perhaps were primary causes of the decline in fervour: the escape from the common life made easy and normal by the proliferation of the obedientiary system, by which the single procurator of the Rule was replaced by numerous officials and sub-officials charged with the administration of estates and funds; the gradual relaxation of the prescriptions of the Rule in the matter of fasting and abstinence, a relaxation not in itself directly evil but indicative of a weakness of faith and spiritual purpose; and, most corrosive of all, the introduction of private ownership and privilege and exemption in numberless occasions of daily life. Small and apparently trivial as all these mitigations may have seemed when regarded individually, and negligible as may have been their effect on this or that fervent individual, they nevertheless despiritualized the whole life of the house, divorced common practice from the precepts of the Rule, and reduced the monk's life from that of a school of the service of God to that of a tolerably easygoing collegiate body. Though an earnest individual under such circumstances might lead an edifying existence, the life as such was no longer of itself a means of sanctification, a way of perfection, a following of Christ.

The friars must be considered apart from the possessioners in any estimate, for their problems were not the same and they present peculiar difficulties to the historian. As they were liable to frequent transference from house to house, we cannot regard any friary as having a moral or spiritual character of its own; moreover, we know next to nothing of any community at any time save for the friaries of Oxford, Cambridge, London and perhaps Canterbury. Certainly what little we know suggests that the friars were intellectually more restless and susceptible of external influence than the monks, and that the rank and file up and down the country had a narrower background and were of simpler, perhaps of

coarser, fibre. There is no clear evidence that the four orders differed greatly among themselves in discipline or characteristics, though there are suggestions that the Dominicans were mentally the most alert. As we have seen, the Roman committee of reform was for extinguishing altogether the conventual or unreformed branches of the Orders, particularly the Franciscan, which was very numerous in Italy. Clearly the friars of all the orders were too numerous in England for good governance, but there is no clear evidence that a large majority were undisciplined beyond all hope. The real difficulty would have been to find for them a focus and agency of reform.

With all these weaknesses and handicaps the English monks and friars had the hard fate of remaining untouched by any reforming hand, any breath of the creative Spirit. From the mid-thirteenth century onwards there was a dearth of founders and saints in England. No new orders like the Servites, no new branch like the Minims or the Carmelite nuns, no reform like that of the Celestines or the Olivetans appeared; no saint arose such as the Catherines of Siena and Genoa, no mystics like Suso and Ruysbroeck, no preachers like Bernardine, Antoninus or John Capistran. The religious of England, separated from the rest of Europe by the sea, by the Hundred Years War, and by nationalist sentiment, produced no champion of their own to renew their youth. The later monastic reforms, several of which, instinct with new life, antedated the Reformation by many years, such as those of S. Giustina di Padova, Bursfelde and Hirschau, and the reforms of the canons and friars, such as Windesheim and the reformed Carmel of Rubeo, together with the Minims and Colettines of France, did not penetrate to this country. Here the old machinery still ran on, though the rhythm was gradually slackening.

The foregoing pages may seem to some readers to be nothing but

> a melancholy tale of things
> Done long ago, and ill done.

They may feel that the splendours of the dawn and noonday have done no more than serve as an introduction to the description of a falling day and lengthening shades. No historian would claim that his picture can adequately reflect the myriad colours of the past, and he may easily falsify its light or its gloom, but it is only right to remember that in the three hundred years before the Reformation the fortunes of monasticism followed those of the whole Western Church. The writer of to-day, aware as he is of the catastrophes and revolutions of the sixteenth century, is justified in seeking to trace in its main lines the gradual deterioration of quality in the institutions and methods and practices of external church life, and in pointing to the abuses of the Curia, to the luxury and venality of Avignon, to the rivalries and jealousies of the Schism, and to the worldliness and ambitions of the popes of the Renaissance, as symptoms and causes of the sickness that attacked head and members. In so doing he does not forget or deny the existence of upright and saintly men and women at Avignon and Rome, and the blameless and devout lives of thousands upon thousands of the faithful, still less the slow but marvellous awakening by which the papacy and the Church in general rose from its long illness with a new vigour. So with the monastic and religious orders there were at all times men and women, both among the superiors and the private religious, of goodwill and spiritual achievement. We may not be able to disguise the general trend of the period with which we have had to deal, but we may remember the words of St. Gregory the Great, echoed by St. Thomas More, that there is little credit for living well in good company, but praise indeed for those who are worthy when all around is ill.

The writer of these pages has often been asked, and has often asked himself, whether the monks of the Tudor Age deserved the hard fate that overtook them. He has tried to answer by presenting the reader of the earlier chapters in this volume with evidence on which to base his judg-ment. It may well be that important pieces have been overlooked, but these chapters contain what seemed, after thirty years of reflection, .to be a representative assemblage. The reader has indeed had before him records of visitations that do little credit to the religious, and has heard the criticisms of contemporaries, including such eminent judges as Erasmus and More, but on the other hand he has entered the cloister of the Charterhouse with Maurice Chauncy, he has seen something of the achievement of Marmaduke Huby and Richard Kidderminster, he has watched Prior More summering and wintering at Worcester and Grimley, and Robert Joseph and his friends discovering Plautus and Virgil. He has seen something of the dignified and richly apparelled liturgy and chant at Durham and Waltham, and has noted the new and beautiful buildings rising at St. Osyth, at Forde and at Westminster, and the words of praise given by their neighbours to many a house great and small.

If the question is still urged, the opinion (it can be no more) of the present writer, if he were to set himself as one surveying the English scene in 1530, would be as follows. In the first place, there were a number of houses — the Charterhouses, Syon, the Observant friaries, many of the larger nunneries, one or two of the cathedral priories, and several other abbeys of the black and white monks—which no temporal or ecclesiastical sovereign would have dreamt of destroying unless he was prepared to deny the right of existence to any monastic house, and to consider solely the cash value of a church and its treasures. Secondly, there was a larger number of houses (though with a smaller aggregate population) whose continued existence served no good purpose whatever. In this category would be found all priories and cells of monks and nuns with less than ten or a dozen inmates, and, in addition, almost all the houses of Augustinian canons. Within no foreseeable future and by no practicable scheme of reform could they have been rehabilitated spiritually. Between these two fairly large groups about which there could have been little serious difference of opinion among men of average insight and probity, there was still a large *bloc* of medium-sized and large houses upon which it would have been difficult to pass judgment. None of them was fervent, but many were harmless and, at least to a good-natured observer from outside, respectable enough to pass muster. The nature of the judgment passed on them would have depended upon the condition of the judge: a tolerant man of the world would have allowed them to continue, a severe spiritual reformer would have found them wanting.

It is not an historian's task to predict the issue of a course of action that never took place, under conditions which were never realized, but if we are allowed, with a momentary flight of fancy, to suppose that in early Tudor England a breach with the papacy and an invasion of Reformed principles and theology were not of themselves inevitable, and that the existence of a strong, prudent and orthodox monarch may be allowed as a hypothesis, it is conceivable that a minister with the powers of Wolsey and the character of a Cisneros[7] or a Pole might, by a judicious combination of suppression and disciplinary reform, have provided the monastic world in England with a purge and a tonic that would have prepared the survivors for the reception of the Tridentine regulations and the constitutions of the contemporary reformed orders of Italy and Spain.

In several chapters of this book the immediate personal and material consequences of the Dissolution have been set out in some detail. It is natural to suppose that the long-term consequences, religious and social, of such a wholesale extinction of a way of life, and such a vast transference of property must have been great indeed. Yet after a century's debate historians are by no means agreed as to the nature or extent of these results. Three hundred years ago the sober and intelligent historian, Thomas

Fuller, tabled a series of consequences based not so much on historical evidence as on his own opinion of the needs and sorrows of his country, and historians almost down to our own day have, whether consciously or not, done little more than echo or embroider his words. There was a time when apologists of the Middle Ages attributed to the Dissolution almost every ill which they deplored in the sixteenth and later centuries: the secular and servile state, the upstart nobility, the parliamentarian gentry, the later oligarchy, pauperism, capitalism, avarice and atheism. More recently still, there has been a tendency to minimize the extent of the revolution. It has been said that the religious were so earthbound that their disappearance left no spiritual void, while at the same time the existing landowners had already such a footing within the monastic estates either as leaseholders or administrators that the Dissolution had little social or economic effect. It would indeed seem true that it is very difficult to distinguish any save the most superficial results in these spheres from those of other disturbing influences of the time, religious, social and economic, but a summary review may not be out of place.

On the spiritual level, the dissolution of the monasteries was not of itself a great catastrophe. By and large the whole body ecclesiastic was lukewarm, and the monasteries had little warmth to spare for others. Nevertheless, their disappearance had considerable consequences. The suppression of the Carthusians, the Bridgettines and the best of the nunneries removed from the national purview an ideal and a practice of life that had always attracted a spiritual *élite* and, in things of the spirit, as in works of art, the best has a value and a price which no quantity, however great, of the mediocre can supply. Next, the witness of Aske[8] and of others shows, what we might expect, that even a tolerably observant religious house could have had an encouraging influence upon good men of the neigh-

[7] The great Spanish reformer, politician, and prelate; Wolsey's contemporary.

[8] Robert Aske (d. 1537), the "captain," or popular leader, of the Pilgrimage of Grace.

bourhood, to say nothing of its real practical use as a school, an almshouse, a bank, or an inn. Thirdly, when the monasteries had been followed to destruction by the colleges, there disappeared from the country almost every home of that rich liturgical life of chant and ceremony of which we have seen glimpses on earlier pages. There remained only the parish church and the minished cathedral; there was no cushion to take the impact of reforming, iconoclastic zeal when it came. Finally, and most important of all, there was the negative result. Good or bad, the monasteries were an important and integral part of the traditional church life of the Middle Ages. Had they stood, the tide of Protestantism in this country would have been, if not halted, at least checked and divided. Their disappearance, especially when their lands and wealth were held by a great number of all the higher classes, rendered any complete revival of the old ways extremely difficult. Without the support and example of the revitalized religious orders on a fairly large scale, Mary, had she lived to be eighty, would have had a hard task to reestablish Catholicism, and any large-scale restitution would have been met with sullen hostility and fear on the part of the landowners of the country. Probably neither Henry VIII nor Cromwell fully realized in this respect what they were doing. They thought of the religious orders primarily as a source of wealth, and only very occasionally as a potential enemy of change. But the monasteries, with all their weaknesses, were more than landowners. They were not indeed, as has sometimes been repeated, fortresses of the papacy, but their existence in a healthy condition was necessary, if not for the *esse,* then at least for the *bene esse,*[9] of a church that was to be part of Catholic Europe, and when they went, something had gone that might have been good or bad, but would never have been Protestant.

On the social and economic level the results are not so clear. There was the great but imponderable loss in things of beauty

devoted, or at least erected, to the glory of God. How great the loss was we can but guess from what remains still in partial use or utterly ruined. Those to whom the great churches and cathedrals stand apart from all other buildings in their power to move and to inspire will never say that enough has been spared. On the purely professional level of architect and craftsman the Dissolution meant the end of an art-form. Gothic art, not yet as strained and flamboyant in England as it was abroad, came to an end as it were overnight, if only because churches were not built any longer. It survived for a generation or two in craft traditions, and then became a curiosity or a survival. Social changes remain hard to assess. A few great families of *nouveaux riches* emerged, and remained for the next half-century near the controls of government, but the new rich were not always new men; for the most part their rise was of a modest landowner to the rank of a magnate, and they were far less numerous than was asserted in the past. They were not precisely a new class or a new way of thought breaking into a charmed circle. The real beneficiaries of the change, once the dust of the suppression settled, were innumerable men of small or moderate fortunes, who bought themselves a small estate or augmented an existing one. It was this multiplication of country landowners that had its effect in time. The map of England was no longer, like those of Catholic France and Germany, marked by numerous islands, the privileged lands great and small of religious corporations. Everywhere laymen were in possession, potential cultured gentlemen of the latter decades of Elizabeth's reign or parliamentarians of a later period. Some of them might well be Catholics, and zealous ones, like the Arundells or the Paulets,[10] but all were, economically speaking, supporters of the "new deal"; all would have been equally apprehensive of a return of

9 "If not for the *being,* then at least for the *well-being . . .*"

10 The Arundells were a famous Cornish family; the Paulets, a prominent political and court-connected family, staunchly adhered to the official religious settlement until the late sixteenth century.

the monks. Here, as often in this matter, the analogy with revolutionary France is close. There also the beneficiaries of the change remained sullen opponents of the old régime, and it needed a papal act of power, which seemed to many as a betrayal of friends, to break the solidarity of the old form of things with the old faith. In England, as we have seen, the pope pronounced early, but, in the shifting policies of the years that followed, the renunciation of claims was allowed to fall into oblivion, and for almost three centuries the rights of the dispossessed remained as a spectre that defied exorcism. In a still more powerful way the ghost of medieval monasticism remained and remains to haunt this island. The grey walls and broken cloisters, the

bare ruin'd choirs, where late the sweet birds sang,

speak more eloquently for the past than any historian would dare, and pose for every beholder questions that words cannot answer.

At the end of this long review of monastic history, with its splendours and its miseries, and with its rhythm of recurring rise and fall, a monk cannot but ask what message for himself and for his brethren the long story may carry. It is the old and simple one; only in fidelity to the Rule can a monk or a monastery find security. A Rule, given by a founder with an acknowledged fullness of spiritual wisdom, approved by the Church and tested by the experience of saints, is a safe path, and it is for the religious the only safe path. It comes to him not as a rigid, mechanical code of works, but as a sure guide to one who seeks God, and who seeks that he may indeed find. If he truly seeks and truly loves, the way will not be hard, but if he would love and find the unseen God he must pass beyond things seen and walk in faith and hope, leaving all human ways and means and trusting the Father to whom all things are possible. When once a religious house or a religious order ceases to direct its sons to the abandonment of all that is not God, and ceases to show them the rigours of the narrow way that leads to the imitation of Christ in His Love, it sinks to the level of a purely human institution, and whatever its works may be, they are the works of time and not of eternity. The true monk, in whatever century he is found, looks not to the changing ways around him or to his own mean condition, but to the unchanging everlasting God, and his trust is in the everlasting arms that hold him. Christ's words are true: He who doth not renounce all that he possesseth cannot be my disciple. His promise also is true: He that followeth me walketh not in darkness, but shall have the light of life.

THE ORIGINS OF PROTESTANTISM
IN ENGLISH SOCIETY

ARTHUR G. DICKENS

As one might infer from his early historical studies of Yorkshire and other northern areas, Professor Arthur G. Dickens was a Yorkshireman by birth (1910). His first-class honors in modern history at Magdalen College, Oxford, launched his career. By 1939 he was University lecturer in sixteenth-century history. After five years of service in the Second World War, Dickens was named professor in the University of Hull. Combining high-level administration there with detailed research, he meticulously studied the society and institutions of the North, on which he wrote numerous articles and monographs as well as a book: *Lollards and Protestants in the Diocese of York*. In 1959 he published an excellent little volume on *Thomas Cromwell* and in 1964 a superb history of *The English Reformation*. In 1962 Dickens became Professor of History, Kings College, London; since July, 1967 he has been Director, Institute of Historical Research, London University.

INTRODUCTION

In a field of historical investigation which involves modern religious controversies, the vice of over-simplification readily asserts itself and the manifold delicate tones of reality are overlaid by the crude black and white of discordant abstractions. That such partisanship has often enfeebled both the selectivity and the generalizing of Reformation historians is now so widely agreed that its grosser excesses seem unlikely to be repeated. Here, nevertheless, has lain only one of the obstacles to sound progress. Working on too ambitious a scale, arbitrarily accepting as typical a few minute sections of the surviving evidence, bemused by the personalities of monarchs and statesmen, emphasizing those facts which happen to fit modern economic and social theories, historians have commonly ended by constructing patterns which bear little relation to the development of the English people as it can be revealed by patient research into personal, local, and regional history. So far as possible, the present writer wants to shun the well-worn themes of high policy and central government, of monarchs, parliaments, statesmen, and theologians. Instead he will take a large area of mid-Tudor England and try to observe, with as many concrete examples as possible, how the Reformation made its initial impacts upon a regional society.

*   *   *

In the politico-religious field the northern Englishman has proved the peculiar victim of simplification. Even in learned accounts, society north of Trent appears uniformly backward-looking, feudal, and monastic in its allegiances, monopolized by stubborn religious conservatism and constantly tempted into treason and rebellion. Both local and regional writings purporting to describe the Reformation too often restrict themselves to the converse theme, that of Reaction, as if the north could boast **no**

From A. G. Dickens, *Lollards and Protestants in the Diocese of York, 1509–1558* (London, 1959), pp. 1, 7–15, 240, 242–46, and 251–52. Reprinted by permission of Oxford University Press, Publisher, and The University of Hull.

history of Protestantism before the seventeenth century. Having formerly helped to swell the output of research upon the Pilgrimage of Grace and the subsequent reactionary movements, I propose in the present essay to skirt this theme and to concentrate upon Lollardy, Protestantism, Edwardian Anglicanism, and other sorts of heretical and Reforming activities manifested in the diocese between the accession of Henry VIII and that of Elizabeth I. I shall avoid also the dissolution of monasteries and chantries, the institutional, economic, and material results of contemporary policy, except in so far as they affected the character and progress of the new doctrines. Significant in their own right, all these matters continue to demand research, yet at this juncture it can do no harm to reassert the primacy of intellectual and spiritual elements in the story of the Reformation. When we leave the sphere of central government and survey the broad fields of English society, the opportunity for this emphasis upon ideas does not diminish. In the diocese of York the materials for such an approach remain considerable, even if they have been little explored. However great their gaps and their unsolved problems, these sources will allow us to grasp the complex character of contemporary religion and to trace some of the channels through which the new opinions were flowing across this large and important sector of English society.

Before embarking upon this regional survey, it would seem desirable to take our bearings, though not to prejudge our findings, by a brief glance at the origins of Protestantism in English society as they are just beginning to emerge in modern scholarship. This theme has little in common with the old Tudor saga: Divorce, Reformation Parliament, Dissolutions, and Prayer Books. Whatever the long-term effects of such high policy, its creative part in the early development of Protestantism has in general been much exaggerated. Again, the ingredients of early Protestantism proved already numerous in the reign of Henry

VIII, yet among them Lutheranism may scarcely be regarded as predominant and Calvinism as yet remained almost negligible. Whatever Gairdner — who knew little about ecclesiastical archives — may have thought, we may nowadays confidently ascribe a role of some importance on the popular level to the still vital force of Lollardy. This "secret multitude of true professors," as Foxe dubs them, continued pertinacious in certain areas during and even beyond the first three decades of the century. In the London diocese, especially in Essex, Bishop Fitzjames prosecuted about 50 Lollards in 1510 and about as many again in 1518. Between 1527 and 1532 his successors Tunstall and Stokesley caused at least 218 heretics to abjure: Colchester shows 20 convicted persons, Steeple Bumpstead 40, and Birdbrook 44. A mixed heresy had now become apparent in the London diocese, yet while Lutheran doctrines emerge in a few cases, the basic and predominant element clearly remains Lollard. Another classic locality of the old English heresy was the Chilterns area, especially around Amersham and Buckingham, where about 45 cases were presented to Bishop Smyth of Lincoln in 1506–7. His successor Longland organized here in 1521 a major drive which resulted in 50 abjurations and 5 burnings. Longland continued active in later years, notably around 1530. This area connected through a number of scattered communities in the Thames Valley with others in Berkshire, Wiltshire, and the Cotswolds. At Newbury, six or seven score heretics are said by Foxe to have abjured together some time during the early years of the century. The final centre lay in south-west Kent, in the clothing towns of Tenterden, Cranbrook, and Benenden. In 1511 some 46 Kentish Lollards were denounced to Archbishop Warham, 5 being burned, the rest abjuring. Between these various groups some links obviously existed: Thomas Man, burned at Smithfield in 1518, had moved about instructing Lollard communities in East Anglia, the Chilterns, the Thames Valley, and Newbury.

Late Lollardy appealed chiefly to working-class people, especially to cloth-workers, who were mobile, but worked in compact communities with an old and fiercely independent tradition deriving from medieval town-life. In his detailed lists, Foxe also mentions tailors, shoemakers, carpenters, wheelwrights, and other small tradesmen and artisans. Mainly in the London diocese, there appear a very few merchants, friars, secular priests, and professional men.

What, by this time, were Lollards believing and teaching? Sensibly, if briefly, Foxe summarizes their heresies: "In four principal points they stood against the Church of Rome: in pilgrimage, in adoration of saints, in reading of Scripture Books in English and in the carnal presence of Christ's body in the Sacrament." These four points merely represent some of the commoner positions. The beliefs charged against any given Lollard do not necessarily include them and may include many others. In Morton's[1] archiepiscopal register, a carpenter of the diocese of Bath and Wells admitted in 1491 to denying Transubstantiation, Baptism, the Confessional, obeisances to the cross, and, curiously, damnation for sin, "for then Criste must nedis dampne his owne flessh and blode that he toke of the Virgin Mary." The same register gives the abjurations of two priests in the diocese of Salisbury under the year 1499. They had disbelieved in Transubstantiation, and had thought "that it is no nede to be shrevin to a prest or to any other mynestre of the Chirch, but that it is inowgh to be aknowyng to God and to be sory for the synne, being in wil to returne no more to the sinne." In addition, they had held that images should not be worshipped or pilgrimages undertaken, "that the Pope is antecrist," and "that prestes and bysshoppes have no more auctorite thenne a nother laymann that folowith the teching and the good conversacioun of the Appostolles." Finally, they had supposed "that the curses

and other sentences of the Chirch be of noone effect."

Amongst these varied positions, the denial of Transubstantiation was one which brought the severest and most frequent danger to the Lollards; it sprang from the late doctrine of Wyclif himself and from Wyclifite books like the *Wycket*, that favourite *vade mecum* of late Lollardy. The struggle with heresy continued to centre around the mass both in Henrician and Marian times; it tempted the heretics into crudely materialist denials and their orthodox persecutors into crudely materialist affirmations, distasteful alike to modern Catholics and Protestants. In the preoccupation of our York documents with this theme of Transubstantiation we shall witness only one small facet of an unimaginably complex and widespread European controversy, the full implications of which are seldom satisfactorily comprehended by modern historians. Readers tempted to suppose that the cases in episcopal registers or in the pages of Foxe involve a simple dichotomy of believer versus non-believer may find food for thought in the fact that Christopher Rasperger published in 1577 a book discussing no less than two hundred interpretations which had been placed on the text, *This is my body*.

Though so many cases of Lollardy are recorded during the first quarter of the sixteenth century, modern researchers are unlikely to approach any statistical estimate of the problem, for long experience had made the Lollards adepts in the art of concealment. Moreover, very few sought martyrdom; they come to light through their abjurations rather than through their sufferings. A little is known concerning their relations with Friar Barnes[2] and with other early disseminators of Lutheran ideas and of Tyndale's New Testament. In one recorded confession, Essex Lollards are seen visiting Barnes in London with their old manuscript English Testaments and then being sold Tyndale's up-to-date publication

[1] Cardinal John Morton (?1420–1500), Archbishop of Canterbury and one of Henry VII's chief ministers.

[2] Robert Barnes, a Cambridge don, Protestant, and martyr.

by the enterprising friar. And though the Cambridge intellectuals who first took up Lutheran and Zwinglian doctrines owed little to Lollardy, their allies the "Christian Brethren," who financed early Lutheran bookselling in England, apparently included men of Lollard affiliations. Even Little Bilney[3] of Cambridge preached to East Anglian Lollard communities. During the 1530's there grew a merging tendency between the old and the new movements. Nevertheless, if the Lollard element gained stiffening from the Continent, it preserved many of its original characteristics throughout the reign of Henry VIII and even beyond. Its social ethos and its doctrines had relatively little in common with moderate Lutheranism, the sacramental and justificatory tenets of which stood at variance with those of Lollardy.

A continental movement much nearer to Lollardy was Anabaptism, which certainly infiltrated from the Netherlands during the thirties. The numerous "Dutch" heretics burned or charged in England, the denunciations of Anabaptism in proclamations and in sermons by conservative Protestants like Latimer, may nevertheless encourage an overestimate of its effects in this country. The unwary might easily mistake Lollardy for Anabaptism. Between two such many-sided and amorphous attacks upon tradition, common doctrines necessarily existed, the most important being a denial of Transubstantiation. There were, indeed, few orthodox religious and social traditions unsubjected at some stage or other to Anabaptist attack. In examining "Dutch" heretics in the diocese of York, we shall certainly need to approach them with an open mind and without the assumption that every "Dutch" heretic was a recent immigrant who had learned his theology in Anabaptist circles abroad, and had imbibed nothing from his English environment.

The remaining ingredients of early pop-

ular Protestantism are too obvious to require detailed description. Concerning the wide dissemination and profound influence of Tyndale's New Testament there can be no doubt. It supplied a vital link between these varied movements, since it enormously facilitated vernacular Bible-study by laymen and women. What inspiration to heroism, what intellectual dangers were entailed by that exhilarating pursuit in an atmosphere of personal discovery and conviction, these are things our own age finds it increasingly hard to imagine. And not far from Tyndale stood Frith, whose violent attack upon Transubstantiation, published already in 1533, soon obtained widespread acceptance in England and supplied fresh weapons to this important section of the old Lollard armoury. The great influence of publicists found acknowledgement in a number of proclamations by an alarmed government. Even the Pilgrims of Grace gave them a prominent place among their grievances. "To have the heresies of Luther, Wyclif, Husse, Melangton, Elicampadus,[4] Burcerus, Confessa Germanie, Apologia Melanctonis, the works of Tyndall, of Barnys, of Marshall, Raskell,[5] Saynt Germayne[6] and other such heresy of Anabaptist destroyed." This list does not, however, suggest that its compilers had any close knowledge of the continental works, and may well have been based upon hearsay and upon the more elaborate lists of prohibited foreign books such as that drawn up at the instigation of the bishops in 1529. After the brief "liberal" interval of the later thirties, the government continued to pay tribute to the great influence of books and naturally enough came to see that the English-language publications formed the key to the situation. In an entry for the year

---

[3] Thomas Bilney, an iconoclast and disbeliever in Purgatory, one of a number of radical early English Protestants; martyred despite his orthodoxy in matters related to the Mass, papal powers, etc.

[4] For Oecolampadius, the early German reformer.

[5] John Raskell, printer and reformer, died in prison in 1536.

[6] Christopher St. German, legal writer and controversialist, one of a number of reform-minded propagandists employed by Thomas Cromwell in the 1530's.

1546 the London diarist Wriothesley[7] provides a characteristic list of the authors then judged to exert lively influence, at least in the London area:

The seventh daie of Julie was proclamation made in the cittie of London with a trompett and an harold-at-arms, with the serjeant-at-armes of the cittie and one of the clarkes of the Papers, for certaine Englishe bookes which contain pernitious and detestable errors and heresies to be brought in by the last daie of August next coming, the names be theise: the text of the New Testament of Tindales or Coverdales translation: the bookes of Frith, Tindalle, Wyckliffe, Joy, Roy, Basiley, Barnes, Coverdale, Tourner, and Tracye, which bookes after the bringinge unto the mayor or bishopp shal be brent, as further by the said proclamation doeth appeare.

Apart from these personal and particular influences, the tide of anti-clericalism enveloped devout and profane, Protestant and Catholic, rich and poor alike. It was the common heritage of Europe in the age of Erasmus, but it reached a new intensity in England with the Hunne crisis of 1514–15 and again during the ministry of Wolsey, whose career brought clerics themselves to the point of anti-clericalism. In the north it was not lacking, even at the height of the Pilgrimage of Grace. In the violent aversion of some provincial heretics to the confessional we shall see but one of its many manifestations. Alongside it, there appears what modern conservatives sometimes call the "tavern-unbelief" of the age: the questioning attitude of the sceptical, materially-minded layman confronted by the more "difficult" doctrinal demands of the Church. This factor did not produce martyrs, but it projected not a few people into the ecclesiastical courts on charges of heresy. Indeed, the line which divides it from positive Lollardy and Protestantism is not invariably easy to draw. Some of the martyrs themselves evinced a straightforward intellectual inability to accept the

miracle of Transubstantiation. In the present writer's view, it is by no means fanciful, when reading certain pages of Foxe, to feel appreciably nearer to the age of Voltaire than elsewhere in our sixteenth-century literature. These elements must again be distinguished from the doctrine which thinkers so diverse as Frith[8] and Thomas Starkey[9] derived from Melanchthon: that many hitherto accepted beliefs and observances are neither scriptural nor necessary to salvation, but mere *adiaphora,* or things indifferent. During the thirties adiaphorism can have had few repercussions outside educated circles, but it was destined to become a pillar of Anglicanism and to be enshrined in nos. XX and XXXIV of the Thirty-nine Articles. The earliest stages of English Protestantism could thus, unlike most of the later stages, become the subject of fascinating chapters in the pre-history of both religious toleration and Rationalism. Mid-Tudor disbelief thus consisted of numerous and most heterogeneous elements, between which the orthodox clergy themselves seldom troubled to make nice distinctions. For example, the great list of *mala dogmata* compiled by the convocation of 1536 deserves much more careful analysis than it has received. Some of the heresies here listed could have a straightforward Lutheran origin; many more unquestionably derive from Lollardy; a few might come from either, while yet others might be either Anabaptist or Lollard. Here also are examples of the popular materialist scepticism, perhaps representing crude derivatives of Anabaptist or Lollard heresies. All these aspects of the repertoire we shall soon encounter in the diocese of York.

Concerning the influence of the contemporary social and economic patterns which underlay these intellectual developments, there can be no exact judgements. Histo-

---

[7] Charles Wriothesley, cousin of the politician Sir Thomas.

[8] John Frith, another Cambridge Protestant martyr.

[9] The author of the famous humanist *Dialogue between Master Lupset and Cardinal Pole,* he was the greatest of the Cromwellian expositors of reform ca. 1533–36.

rians who reject economic totalitarianism are unlikely to accord them more than an auxiliary role, since, with many foreign examples in mind, it requires no great effort of imagination to envisage the spread of Protestantism in a society and an economy very differently organized from those of Tudor England. Nevertheless, certain favourable secular patterns undoubtedly accelerated the rise of the new opinions. The weaving community of Hadleigh in Suffolk seemed to Foxe "in respect of scriptural knowledge rather a university of the learned than a town of cloth-making or labouring people." Cloth-workers were now especially exposed to foreign immigrant influence; it will also be observed how personal mobility inside their industry could bring the new opinions out of East Anglia into Yorkshire. In later years the fierce Protestantism of the former was to have its Yorkshire counterpart in the extensive parish of Halifax. Again, it is difficult to exaggerate the role of common lawyers in the development of anti-clericalism. During the fourteenth and fifteenth centuries they had occasionally betrayed their ambitions to bring all ecclesiastical jurisdiction into the uncertain boundaries of the statutes of Praemunire. The judges figured prominently amongst those who attacked the church courts and clerical privilege in the crisis of 1515. Christopher St. German was an eminent theorist and Simon Fish a scurrilous pamphleteer, yet in 1529–31 these two struck the harshest blows at the Church, and both were common lawyers. The numerous provincial gentry who went up to the Inns of Court thus moved instantly into a world of advanced ideas in the heart of the metropolis. Even in the heart of York we must be prepared to meet a few recorded examples of gentlemen who thus encountered the New Learning while in search of this secular instruction. Finally, we cannot doubt the connexions of the merchant-classes and the ports with both English and continental Reformers. In May 1530 Bishop Nix of Norwich denounced the prevalence of heretical litera-

ture in English and added, "the gentlmen and the commenty be not greatly infect; but marchants and suche that hath ther abyding not ferre from the see." This pattern finds illustration with the London–Antwerp group of Protestant merchants and with the active circulation of Protestant literature in Bristol. Likewise Roger Dichaunte, merchant of Newcastle, abjured before Bishop Tunstal the opinions that the mass "crucifiethe Christe of newe," that "man haith no fre will," that "every christen man is a preste," that "every preste myght and ought to be maryed," and that "the lyfe of relygiose men lyvinge in their cloysters is but ypocrisye." The second of these beliefs presumably indicates continental influence. We might reasonably expect to find some traces of a similar process in Hull and York.

All these and other factors of the social and economic background did no more than facilitate the advance of ideas already strong, militant, and intrinsically attractive, yet their significance cannot be dismissed as negligible. The soil was all the more speedily and broadly irrigated, since these old and well-cut channels lay in the path of the rising flood.

The foregoing paragraphs represent merely a few clues and pointers derived from the sketchy sources already at our disposal. They are far from being a definite "national picture" of early English Protestantism, since this picture has still to be built up by painstaking research into regional evidence.

*   *   *

CONCLUSION

The most interesting and novel part of our inquiry has concerned heresy and Protestantism amongst the common people and middle classes. We have tried to show that historians need not adopt a defeatist attitude when questioned as to what the early Reformation meant in the minds of obscure working-class and middle-class people. From the York diocesan records and from some other sources we have extracted and summarized details of proceedings against some thirty-two named heretics in the time of Henry VIII and against about forty-five others during the reign of Mary. The numerical significance of such extant cases depends on our estimate of certain underlying problems. In the first place we may well ask whether they represent all or almost all of the actual heresy-trials conducted during these reigns, or whether there are likely to have been many more, the records of which have perished. So far as the Council in the North and the Six Articles persecution are concerned, we can speak with little precision. The entry-books of the Council have perished, and its surviving reports are in some years very infrequent. We have no reason, however, to suppose that it was constantly dealing with heretics. ... Altogether, though few dioceses can boast at this period so remarkable a coverage as that at York, we must reckon with the likelihood of a number of lost cases of heresy. The present writer nevertheless finds it difficult to suppose these so numerous or so significant as to disturb the main lines of the picture already presented.

Against the generally conservative background of the thirties, forties, and fifties, Lollard and continental Protestant notions were more widely disseminated in the diocese of York than it has hitherto been customary, or indeed possible, to suppose. The case for this view does not, of course, depend upon arguments indicating the incompleteness of our documentation of prosecutions for heresy. Even if some unforeseen discoveries enabled us to double the number of such recorded prosecutions, the real extent and nature of heresy and sub-heresy would not become much more apparent. Likewise no one would claim that the recorded Elizabethan prosecutions for Romanist recusancy revealed the whole extent of Catholic and traditionalist beliefs in the population. In both these fields the surviving records resemble the visible portions of an iceberg, but with this difference, that no constant factor enables the observer to calculate the dimensions of the part submerged. With our Lollards and early Protestants, this task presents unknowns even greater than those surrounding Romanism under Elizabeth, since recusancy and noncommunicancy at least involved public acts and became subject to elaborate reports and censuses. In the case of mid-Tudor heresy, no element of potential treason brought into play the full resources of the state-machine; with reasonable caution, friendly neighbours, and an unobservant parish priest, many a man may have entertained heterodox views without grave risk of prosecution. We have seen how laymen tended to conceal other laymen attacked by priests. At Hull and Halifax gross offences against the sacrament escaped unpunished, though their perpetrators must have been widely known. Tudor neighbourliness might not indeed extend far. It apparently did not extend to offences by aliens or by strangers from other parts of England, who form, at least in the thirties, a suspiciously large section of the defendants in court.

A far more important consideration lies, however, in the very nature of mid-Tudor heresy. It was so often fragmentary, fleeting, and elusive: it involved a climate of opinion rather than a number of specific heretics, each with an integrated theology and under the guidance of educated leaders. When in 1542 the parish clerk of Topcliffe refused Confession because "there was a saying in the country that a man might lift up his heart and confess himself to God Almighty and need not be confessed at a priest," he proceeded to swear, perhaps quite honestly, that he could not recall the names of those who said this. He was reporting a phenomenon which could not effectively be tracked down by authority or one which we may now turn into statistical surveys. Heretical ideas floated freely about the country and were held — with most varying degrees of conviction and piety — by people who did not for a moment claim to be theologians and had no intention of going to the stake. From the viewpoint of orthodoxy, herein lay the formidable character of the movement; it was a hydra which survived attack by the normal repressive weapons. On the opposite front, Henry VIII found papalism a relatively simple animal; it could be checked by a strictly limited number of decapitations.

These interesting qualities the rise of non-Catholic beliefs must have owed in large part to its Lollard basis. Scholars who seek an historical understanding of the English Reformation would be wise to think a little less about Bucer, Bullinger, and even Cranmer, and somewhat more in terms of a diffused but inveterate Lollardy revivified by contact with continental Protestantism. This hypothesis finds powerful support in the records of the diocese of York. Here, it may reasonably be suggested, we witness the later repercussions of that Lollard revival which had manifested itself in southern England during the first three decades of the century. Several well-documented heresy cases of the late twenties and thirties prove indistinguishable from those of the early years, when Luther and Zwingli had not yet even begun to formulate their doctrines. In substance and in name, Lollardy continued into the reign of Mary, increasingly merging with the newer Protestant doctrines, yet continuing throughout the diocese to colour the popular heresy with its unmistakable tints. Wherever we search at these levels of society, we detect the late-medieval English heresy. Some of the Henrician offenders, for example, were "Dutchmen" by origin, yet every one of their numerous and carefully recorded beliefs has its Lollard precedents, while not one of them can claim exclusively Lutheran, Anabaptist, or other continental antecedents. Under Henry VIII the demonstrable infiltration of foreign Protestantism to form a mixed heresy on this popular level occurs only in the cases of a tiny handful of semi-educated offenders. Lollardy had on the whole survived through its resilience; it had its heroes, but the great majority of its adherents were not superhuman figures drawn from the pages of Foxe. . . . The average neo-Lollard or Lollard Protestant behaves

quite otherwise when we meet him in the Court of Audience at York. He is a man of ordinary courage; he trembles at his danger, makes excuses, displays penitence, submits to instruction, does penance, and is thenceforth careful to keep his convictions to himself. . . .

The character of this native medieval tributary to the English Reformation finds excellent illustration in the records at York. The popular heresy is directed against the supposed *ministerium mechanicum* of hierarchic Christianity. Its nature compares closely with the summary attempted by Foxe. It takes three chief courses. It assiduously attacks saint-worship, images, relics, holy-bread, holy-water, and the attribution of a sacred character to buildings, places, and things. Again, it denounces Confession to priests. Why, asked one young artisan with brutal frankness, why should I confess an affair with a pretty woman to my knavish confessor, who, given the chance, would use her similarly? If, he continued, I believe steadfastly in God, calling to Him with a sorry heart for my offences, God will forgive me. Yet the most vital element in the popular heresy was its denial of the corporal presence of Christ's Body in the eucharist. This was the offence which brought more offenders into serious trouble than any other: if today we still venture to take notice of conscious motivation, we might well urge that the early Reformation-struggle in England was primarily waged not over the royal divorce, the sovereignty of the State, or the possession of the monastic lands, but over the sacrament of the altar. Throughout the heresy cases in the York courts, sacramentarian offences seem to play an increasing part as time passes. Under Henry VIII they occupy the predominant role in rather less than half the cases: under Mary, in considerably more than a half. In both groups the same three denials dominate the popular heresy, while a fourth element, the desire for direct and personal study of the Bible and of its modern commentators, is indeed represented, but only in three or four cases. In the diocese of York we are not ostensibly dealing, even around 1530, with Lollard communities whose life still centred around illicit Bible-reading. So far as this evidence goes, the Lollard tradition had become diffused and sometimes even manifested itself in scepticism rather than in affirmation by the time it began to meet with Tyndale. Its historical importance may lie in the fact that it united with the more worldly types of anti-clericalism to form an extensive platform of critical dissent upon which the various newer movements could build. The discovery that even the society of a northern and conservative shire was to some extent still permeated by a diluted Lollardy seems to provide an important missing link in the history of the English Reformation. It helps to show that the latter did not originate as a mere foreign doctrine imported by a handful of intellectuals and mysteriously imposed by the monarchy against the almost unanimous wishes of a Catholic nation. The foreign seed fell upon a ground prepared for its reception, and prepared by something more than anticlericalism or royal propaganda. Nevertheless, on the basis of our regional examples it might well be questioned whether Lollardy could much longer have retained a recognizable profile had new forces not ranged themselves behind some of its principles and gradually assumed intellectual leadership. Perhaps its emphasis had come to bear too purely upon negations; its clichés, now widely disseminated in society, had too often got into the wrong mouths. At all events, they seem to have harmonized remarkably well with the devastatingly outspoken dissent which has always formed one pole of the Yorkshire temperament, just as an emotional religiosity formed the other.

*   *   *

The foregoing inquiries have enabled us to detect more clearly this heavy groundswell within English society; they have pushed back the beginnings of regional dissent and of religious heterogeneity far behind the Elizabethan age. The Edwardians and the Marians alike failed, it would seem, to hustle the slow bend of new and old forces in the English mind. The spectacular events of 1534–58 still play a large part in the historical textbook, but historians of the English people may increasingly find them superficial, since the origins of religious change occurred much earlier and the really epoch-making developments somewhat later. While, on the one hand, the survival of a diffused Lollardy helps to explain so many features of the mid-Tudor scene, on the other hand the popularization of the newer religions surely cannot be made to precede the middle decades of Elizabeth. Whatever its theological continuities, the vitality of Roman Catholicism had to be re-created in its limited sector of English society by the seminarist invasion of the seventies and eighties. Similarly, Anglicanism cannot claim to date, as a spiritual force amongst the people, from the Prayer Book of 1549 or from the Act of Uniformity ten years later; only the age of Hooker saw it develop an appeal upon a national scale, an ethos extending outside a small cultured circle. At this same period, both inside and outside the national Church, Calvinist puritanism still fought for a following. If all three developed at last into established and unshakeable phenomena amongst Englishmen and Americans, none may claim to be other than a late-comer upon the Tudor scene. The present writer has hitherto conducted detailed religious and literary investigation mainly within the diocese of York: if compelled to establish major landmarks in both these fields of mental history, he would prefer to place the end of the Middle Ages and the rise of modern movements around the eighth decade of the sixteenth century. And he feels no doubt that the thesis might be maintained for other large regions of England. Yet dissent, in the looser sense of the word, had been present long beforehand: it had arisen *pari passu* with the slow breakdown of the medieval synthesis and it broadened into the very *Zeitgeist* of the Tudor age. The pious Nonconformists who hailed Wyclif as the morning star of the Reformation were saying something with profounder implications than they realized.

We have already compared the religious history of the mid-Tudor period with the growth of a forest: if the reader will tolerate one more crude parable, we might also compare it with a lake. It had both muddy shallows and capricious eddies, yet it was fed by rivers and in turn gave birth to other rivers. Of the feeders, the broad stream of medieval orthodoxy and the spectacular but less voluminous cataracts of continental Protestantism have tended to monopolize our vision. The Lollard river, deep, murky, and quiet, has inevitably suffered neglect, since it ran underground and seldom emerged before reaching the lake. As for the effluent rivers, Anglican, Catholic, and puritan, these have now become familiar in outline, though still imperfectly charted around the points where they leave the lake's Elizabethan shores. Yet the foregoing work seeks at least to indicate that we have still much to learn concerning the lake itself, that even now we may gain new knowledge of its actual waters, as distinct from those sedimentary deposits which have become the main preoccupation of twentieth-century map-makers. Beyond that oft-encountered earthiness and disillusion, even mid-Tudor society had its spiritual turmoil and tension, its vast potentialities, and its epoch-making decisions. It forms more than a period of survivals and prehistories; it has a quality of its own which we can best recover by switching to new lines of inquiry and new sources of factual information. It looks after all integral enough to the story of a small but intensely vital nation; a nation which above all others was destined during the subsequent two centuries to revolutionize the prospects of Western Man.

"O THE GREAT JUDGMENTS OF GOD!"

CHRISTOPHER HILL

The current Master of Balliol College, Oxford, went there to study as a young man (b. 1912), stayed as a fellow and tutor, left for the Second World War, and returned as a promising historian in 1945. Since that time he has been University lecturer in sixteenth- and seventeenth-century history there and also had the honor of the Ford's lectureship in 1962. A somewhat controversial figure because of his Marxist persuasions and his persistent exposition of an "economic determinist" position in many of his works, Christopher Hill has written several major books and numerous essays and articles, among the chief of which are: *Economic Problems of the Church, Puritanism and Revolution, Society and Puritanism in Pre-Revolutionary England,* and *The Intellectual Origins of the Puritan Revolution.*

I

THE REFORMATION in England was an act of state. The initiative came from Henry VIII, who wanted to solve his matrimonial problems. The King had the enthusiastic support of an anti-clerical majority in the House of Commons (representing the landed gentry and the merchants) and of the propertied classes in the economically advanced south and east of England. Overt opposition came only from the more feudal north (the Pilgrimage of Grace in 1536). The Reformation was not motivated by theological considerations: Henry VIII burnt Protestants as well as opponents of the royal supremacy. Some supporters of the Reformation were heretics; but the wide expansion of Protestantism in England was a consequence, not a cause, of the Reformation.

This was of course the most important outcome of the English Reformation. But it also had economic and social consequences, which played their part in preparing for the Revolution of 1640–9. The most obvious effect of the Reformation in England was the weakening of the Church as an institution. At the dissolution of the monasteries landed property bringing in a net annual income of over £136,000, and bullion, plate, and other valuables worth possibly £1–1½ million, were taken away from the Church and handed over to laymen of the propertied class. To convey the significance of these figures we may recall that royal revenue from land never exceeded £40,000 a year before 1542.

The Church's loss of economic power brought with it a decline in political power. In Parliament, the removal of abbots from the House of Lords meant that the clerical vote there changed from an absolute majority to a minority. Bishops ceased to be great feudal potentates and sank to even greater dependence on the Crown. Convocation lost its legislative independence. With monastic property the Church lost the right of presentation to some two-fifths of the benefices of the kingdom:[1] this was ultimately to have momentous consequences. The Church also lost a great deal of that vast system of patronage — jobs for

[1] The right to nominate to a vacant church living, or benefice.

laymen no less than for ecclesiastics — which a shrewd observer noted as one of the main sources of strength of the Roman Catholic Church on the continent at the end of the sixteenth century. In addition, the Church lost over £40,000 a year in first-fruits and tenths, and judicial profits (restraint of appeals to Rome). These sums had been drawn out of the kingdom, and so did not benefit the English hierarchy directly: but they added to the wealth, power, and prestige of the international Church, and helped to build up a fund from which the highest dignitaries even of the English Church did not fail to benefit. The transfer of this regular income to the Crown again increased its relative economic power whilst diminishing that of the Church.

This then is the second major economic consequence of the English Reformation: the transfer of wealth and economic influence from the Church to the Crown, and the consequent political subordination of the former. Henry VIII, and later William Cecil, recommended a Reformation to Scotland for precisely this reason. Much of the confiscated property was handed away by the Crown, but little enough of it returned to ecclesiastics or ecclesiastical bodies. The various projects for utilizing parts of the spoil for charitable, educational, or religious purposes came to very little:[2] of the 26 new bishoprics which it was at one time proposed to create, only six were in fact set up, and one of these failed to survive. The subordination of the Church to the Crown remained a fact, and its subordination to the inheritors of its wealth became a possibility.

Who were the inheritors? Here we must distinguish between long-term and short-term consequences. It is clear that, in the first instance, there was nothing revolutionary about the Reformation land transfers, in England as in Germany. It was a shift in the balance of property within the landed ruling class, a land-grabbing opera-

tion of which the immediate beneficiaries were those who were politically influential at the time of the dissolution. Two out of every three peers were granted, or bought, monastic estates: peers, courtiers, royal officials and servants between them account for over two-thirds of the initial recipients. In the seventeenth century it was agreed that nearly all the then members of the peerage held monastic lands.

This was no social revolution. Nevertheless, it marked rather more than a mere shift of landed property, and of all the power and prestige that went with it, from clerical big landowners to lay big landowners. For those who were influential at Henry VIII's Court included many "new men," members of the lesser gentry who had devoted themselves to the royal service: and the Pilgrimage of Grace showed clearly enough that sections of the old aristocracy were out of sympathy with Henry's policy. The Reformation land settlement was part of a shift of power within the landed ruling class, from the great feudal families, with their centrifugal traditions, to the aspiring gentry and new men who were coming up into their places through royal favour. The dissolution of the monasteries takes its place beside the statute of liveries in reducing the social influence of the old aristocracy.

For a monastery was in many ways an asset to the family which had endowed it. It gave the lord and his household free board and lodging whenever he required it. If it held its land by knights' service, this brought in revenue in the form of feudal aids. The founder's heir expected to be consulted before an abbot was elected: this naturally brought financial advantages. These, and other less precisely definable fruits of feudal dependence, were lost at the dissolution, when many of the purchasers became tenants in chief of the Crown. Lord Berkeley is said to have lost 80 knights' fees in this way, "to the value of £10,000 within the compass of few years." It was one of the many blows which that ancient family suffered in the sixteenth century. Peers and gentlemen had held many of the lucrative official posts which

[2] Recent writers on Reformation and education have considerably modified this view, especially Joan Simons (see Suggestions for Further Reading).

were at the disposal of monasteries. Moreover the religious life had offered an easy and profitable career to younger sons of well-connected families, and nunneries what Milton ungallantly described as "convenient stowage for their withered daughters." The dissolution set the aristocracy new problems in raising marriage portions and dowries, at a time when prices were rising on the matrimonial market. It may have stimulated that tendency to marriage between aristocratic and merchant families which becomes noticeable at about this time.

Sir Thomas Smith observed in Elizabeth's reign that "suche younger brothers as were wonte to be thruste into Abbayes, there to live an idle life, sith that is taken from them muste now seeke some other place to live in." The loss of monastic jobs was not compensated for, in England, by the development of a standing army officered by the gentry. Hence the portionless younger son of good family becomes the familiar problem child of Elizabethan literature. Hence too the prominence of poor younger brothers in the more speculative types of overseas adventure, whether in Ireland or in the New World. In this way too the dissolution contributed indirectly to the growth of free enterprise.

The monasteries, Fuller tells us, were "a great cause of the long continuance of the English nobility in such pomp and power, as having then no temptation to torture their tenants with racking of rents, to make provision for their younger children." It has often been suggested that the purchasers of monastic lands introduced a new commercial spirit into agriculture; but this general weakening of the position of the old landowners would, as Fuller suggests, have worked in the same direction. Monasteries had also offered a cheap way of pensioning off superannuated civil servants or dependants of founders' families, who after the dissolution had swept away such "corrodies" became a burden on the family (or the parish).

So for a section of the aristocracy the Reformation brought economic loss, though not for the class as a whole. We should be very careful not to see anything "antifeudal" in this process. Indeed, in a sense the dissolution led to an intensification of feudalism, since it multiplied tenures in chief. Before the Reformation it was mainly great landowners, ecclesiastical and lay, who held by knights' service. But the splitting up of monastic estates scattered what Spelman[3] called "the leprosy of this tenure" throughout the kingdom. The Court of Wards had to be established to deal with the spate of new financial business coming in to the Crown. Heraldic Visitations took on a new significance from Henry VIII's reign, not only because of the increasing number of *parvenus* but also because the monasteries had hitherto acted as genealogical depositories.

II

Yet the monarchy was not permanently strengthened by the Reformation. The ecclesiastical property which passed to it was soon dissipated. Henry VIII built a great fleet and fought wars in France out of the proceeds of the dissolution; Elizabeth sold nearly all the remaining monastic lands to pay for the Irish war at the end of her reign. So the lands found their way on to the market; and the tax-payers did not have to foot the whole bill for national defence. The men of property benefited both ways.

In the short run, then, the Reformation strengthened the position of the lay landed ruling class as a whole, though it weakened some of those members of it hitherto most powerful. Even where the immediate recipient of monastic lands passed them on by sale, he almost certainly made a handsome profit on the transaction. The position of the Crown was temporarily strengthened, not only by monastic estates but also by the steady revenue from first-fruits and tenths and by the accession of political strength through the royal supremacy. It looked as though a sound economic foundation had been laid for English absolutism.

3 Henry Spelman, the famous lawyer, politician, and antiquarian of the Civil War era.

But we speak in abstractions: "Crown," "royal supremacy." Edward VI's reign shows us these terms translated into social reality. "The Crown" retained its initiative during the minority of the King: the "royal supremacy" was used to continue the plunder of the Church for the benefit of Court aristocrats. Under Mary "the Crown" was unable to undo the economic consequences of the Reformation. The process continued under Elizabeth, on a smaller scale but for the same ends: "the Crown" was a funnel through which the wealth of the Church (bishops' lands in Elizabeth's reign) was drained off into the pockets of courtiers.

There were limits to the process, but they were not imposed either by the greed of the aristocracy or the willingness of the Crown to satisfy it. They were imposed by quite a different consideration. The Church's wealth and prestige could not be reduced beyond a certain point without seriously impairing its effectiveness as a buttress of the social order. The attack on Church property had been accompanied by the abolition of confession, penance and sale of indulgences, and by destruction of altars, windows, statues, etc., all of which reduced popular respect for the more mysterious powers of the Church, its sacraments, and saints. The limits were very nearly reached in Edward VI's reign, and this led all those who opposed social revolution to support the Marian reaction. Elizabeth's ecclesiastical *via media* was not entirely voluntary: she was left with very restricted ground for manoeuvre. By the time that James succeeded her, a positive policy of protection and support for the Church was the order of the day: "no bishops, no king, no nobility."

It is indeed one of the many paradoxes of the English Reformation that in temporarily solving the economic problems of the ruling class it gave a stimulus to ideas which were ultimately to overthrow the old order. The Church was permanently weakened. Such authority as it henceforth held it derived from the Crown: bishops

and kings stood or fell together. The critical ideas put about to justify the dissolution of the monasteries reverberated on long after the monks were forgotten. Henry VIII allowed the Bible to be translated into English, and a century later the soldiers of the New Model Army marched into battle against his successor singing psalms. In the short run it was good diversionist tactics to blame the monks and friars for all the economic ills the poor suffered: but when monks and friars had been replaced by lay landlords and poverty remained, new questions began to be asked.

In all spheres, if we extend our vision to the middle of the next century, the long-term outcome of the Reformation was the opposite of that intended by the Machiavellians who introduced it. Charles I's Secretary of State, the near-papist Windebanke, pointed out to the representative of the Pope in England the historical irony of the situation. "Henry VIII committed such sacrilege by profaning so many ecclesiastical benefices in order to give their goods to those who, being so rewarded, might stand firmly for the king in the lower house; and now the king's greatest enemies are those who are enriched by these benefices. . . . O the great judgments of God!" The overthrow of papal authority by Henry VIII thus looks forward to the civil war and the execution of Charles I. The royal supremacy yielded place to the sovereignty of Parliament, and that to demands for the sovereignty of the people. The plunder of the Church by the landed ruling class stimulated the development of capitalism in England. The attack on Church property by the rich led to a questioning of property rights in general.

III

In the first instance, then, the wealth of the monasteries passed to a narrow group. Most of the properties were resold, and by the end of the century had come into the possession of gentlemen or monied men from the towns. The dissolution caused no social revolution. The social revolution that *was* taking place arose independently. It was caused by the rise of capitalism, notably in the clothing and extractive industries, and in agriculture.

In all sorts of indirect ways the Reformation contributed to this development. The dissolution indeed had become possible because the monasteries were ceasing to fulfil functions recognized by the propertied classes as useful. Their days of primacy in agricultural production were over: for the most part they had become parasitic rentiers. Economic initiative passed to the local gentry, who at the dissolution often purchased estates which they were already farming. The rich had ceased to endow new monasteries. The main interest of those stories of corruption and immorality in the abbeys which were used to justify the dissolution is not as evidence of fact but as evidence of what public opinion was prepared to believe.

The original recipient of monastic property, if he sold, would receive a windfall lump sum, which he might fritter away as income, but which alternatively he might invest in improved farming methods. Many middlemen, merchants and others, bought in order to re-sell, making a profit in the process. The ultimate purchaser was by definition a monied man, and so possibly a man of enterprise and ability. In nine cases out of ten he no doubt bought for reasons of social prestige rather than to make profits. But he had to recover his purchase money: he was likely to be a man of business habits, who would at least look to his profit and loss account more closely than his monastic predecessors. In this whole process we are considering very early beginnings. For one William Stumpe who converted Malmesbury Abbey into a factory, there were no doubt scores of Eliots and Cromwells and Fairfaxes who turned abbeys into country houses: and the Corporation of Lynn was equally exceptional in transforming an impropriate church into a factory. But the important thing for our purpose *is* the exception, the new tendency. Glastonbury Abbey became a wor-

sted manufactory, Rotherham College a malt-house. At Grimsby a friary was turned into a storehouse. In London, glass factories were established at the Black, White, and Crutched Friars, a storehouse at Greyfriars and at the Priory of St. John of Jerusalem; New Abbey, East Smithfield, became a biscuit factory and storehouse; the Minories was converted into an armoury and workhouses. Immigrants settled in vacated monastic sites: Stowe dated the expansion of the City's population from the expulsion of the monks. The Marian exiles brought back new industrial techniques.

Many monasteries had been enclosing landlords, but on balance their methods of estate management had been conservative. The properties of St. Albans Abbey, valued at £2,510 at the dissolution, were worth 80 times as much to the lay inheritors a century later. There is undoubtedly a connection between the land transfers, the advent of new purchasers anxious to recoup themselves, and the extension of enclosure for sheep farming. We need not idealize the abbeys as lenient landlords to admit some truth in contemporary allegations that the new purchasers shortened leases, racked rents, and evicted tenants. William Stumpe was one of the many who did this. "Do ye not know," said John Palmer to a group of copyholders he was evicting, "that the king's grace hath put down all houses of monks, friars and nuns, therefore now is the time come that we gentlemen will pull down the houses of such poor knaves as ye be?" Whether the purchasers farmed the land themselves, or leased it out to a man prepared to pay a higher rent, is immaterial for our purpose: the new tendency was accelerated, at any rate in the south and east of England.

We may also note the families whose wealth was raised by coal or iron which had previously been in the possession of monasteries — the Herberts, Lowthers, Cliffords, Riddells, Lilburnes, Sidneys. The purchasers stimulated development by bringing fresh minds and fresh capital into the coal fields. The transfer of ecclesiastical properties seems to have had a similar effect on the metallurgical and salt industries. Many lesser families acquired small realizable windfalls in the shape of building stone or lead from abbey buildings, or timber from abbey lands. A further stimulus to production came from the retention in England of sums hitherto exported to Rome, and the consequent expansion of government expenditure, notably on shipbuilding and armaments. Monasteries had acted as deposit banks: their place had now to be filled by more enterprising institutions. When the government sold former monastic lands it was again largely to finance expenditure on armaments.

The cumulative economic effects of the exactions of the pre-Reformation Church were pointed out by William Tyndale. Wills, tithes, fees, mortuaries; "Then beadrolls. Item chrysome, churchings, banns, weddings, offering at weddings, offering at buryings, offering to images, offering of wax and lights, which come to their vantage; besides the superstitious waste of wax in torches and tapers throughout the land. Then brotherhoods and pardoners. What get they also by confessions? . . . Soul-masses, dirges, month-minds, year-minds, All-souls-day, and trentals. The mother church, and the high altar, must have somewhat in every testament. Offerings at priests' first masses. Item, no man is professed, of whatsoever religion [i.e. religious order] it be, but he must bring somewhat. The hallowing, or rather conjuring of churches, chapels, altars, super-altars. . . . Then book, bell, candle-stick, organs, chalice, vestments, copes, altar-cloths, surplices, towels, basins, ewers, ship [incense-holder], censer, and all manner ornament, must be found for them freely; they will not give a mite thereunto. Last of all, what swarms of begging friars are there! The parson sheareth, the vicar shaveth, the priest polleth, the friar scrapeth, and the pardoner pareth; we lack but a butcher to pull off the skin. . . . If the tenth part of such tyranny were given the king yearly, and laid up in the shire-towns, against the realm had need,

what would it grow to in certain years?"

The economic case against the Church and its courts could be illustrated from any number of contemporary sources. The abolition of indulgences, pilgrimages, friars, and of a number of fees, created at least the possibility that money spent on such forms of conspicuous waste might be devoted to productive purposes. "If it were against the commandement of God, to have images in the Churches," said a Spaniard in Mexico to his English captive in 1556, "then he had spent a great deale of money in vaine." After the Reformation, a much smaller proportion of the English national income than, say, the Spanish, was required to maintain ecclesiastics who were unproductive consumers. Although monks and nuns were pensioned, monastic servants were thrown upon the labour market and helped to keep wages down, to the advantage of industry.

The fact that Protestantism was a cheaper religion than Catholicism became a seventeenth-century commonplace. Saints' days hindered men "from the necessary works of their callings," said Nicholas Bownde in 1608; "which hath moved the Reformed Churches . . . to cut off many that were used in time of Popery." In 1624 James Howell contrasted Protestant England with Catholic Spain in this respect: in Spain, he calculated, days amounting to more than five months in the year were dedicated to some saint or other and kept festival: "a religion that the London apprentices would like well." Colbert succeeded in reducing saints' days in France to 92 *per annum* in 1666: so Howell's estimate was not so wildly out. A late seventeenth-century English economist calculated that every holiday lost £50,000 to the nation. That was the new attitude with a vengeance.

We need not inquire how satisfactorily the monasteries had functioned as agencies of poor relief, nor ask what had happened to the impotent poor in the 8,000 odd parishes in which there had been no monastery. Individual hospitality on the grand scale was falling into disuse by the time of the dissolution. In the north of England the abbeys may still have had their uses: some of the rebels of 1536 appear to have thought so. But monastic charity was unorganized and indiscriminate, and may well have stimulated vagabondage and idleness. The causes of poverty and vagrancy lay in the deeper social transformation we have been considering, of which the transfer of monastic lands was but a small contributory part. But the dissolution did remove one possible piece of machinery for coping with the problem of poor relief on the new scale required. In Ireland the great Earl of Cork was able to convert two friaries into houses of correction, "in which the beggarly youth are taught trade"; and in seventeenth-century France Colbert had schemes for using religious foundations to employ the poor. On the other hand the Protestant social conscience, and the Protestant respect for labour, produced a new attitude towards beginning by regarding it as a social problem, and no longer as either a holy state or a divine necessity. The act for dissolution of the monasteries provided for the maintenance by the purchasers of traditional hospitality. But the lands changed hands many times, and might be subdivided. As the economic and moral climate changed, the charitable obligations laid on the purchasers were disregarded, and the real burden of the dissolution was placed on the poorest classes. With monastic property the new owners usually acquired the right to collect tithes and to present ministers: by the end of the sixteenth century five out of every six benefices in the country were in lay patronage. At the manorial level, a *cuius regio eius religio* system was established in England. This ensured that those divisions inside the landed class which developed later in the sixteenth century would be reflected in the clergy: the Puritan ministers could never have formed the influential group they did had it not been for the support of lay patrons.

IV

Finally the Reformation created a vested interest in Protestantism. This was comparable in its effects, it has been suggested, to the foundation of the Bank of England a century and a half later. When the elder Sir Richard Grenville[4] told Thomas Cromwell that he would like to buy monastic lands, in order that in religious matters his heirs might be of the same mind for their own profit, he was giving naïve expression to an important truth. "Butter the rooks' nests," Sir Thomas Wyatt[5] said to Henry VIII when the latter was worried about the dangers of revolution, "and they will never trouble you." The wisdom may have come after the event; but that was certainly the effect of the dispersal of the lands. It was a Lancashire proverb that the Botelers of Bewsey were the only landowners in the county whose Protestantism was not economically determined by the possession of monastic estates.

The vested interest so created proved too strong for Queen Mary. Yet her attempt at restoration of monastic lands, and the Pope's refusal to confirm her acceptance of the Reformation land settlement, left a deep sence of insecurity, and a terror of Popery, in all holders of church estates. In 1563 the Speaker of the House of Commons told Elizabeth that Papists aimed at "the destruction of goods, possessions, and bodies" no less than at "thraldom of the souls" of Englishmen. Stephen Gardiner and Mary had reversed Henry VIII's policy of neglecting the old nobility for "new men." Elizabeth laid herself open to Catholic taunts that she revived her father's policy in this respect. But the families which Mary had restored were solidly Catholic: the rising of 1569 was led by the great feudal houses of the north and directed against the new men. Mary Queen of Scots succeeded to the leadership of this party: her victory, a Member of Parliament declared in 1572, would mean that all our lands will be lost, all our goods forfeit. The Reformation, the official historian of the

[4] Father of the Elizabethan sea-dog and captain of the *Revenge*.

[5] The courtier and poet.

Long Parliament noted, also engaged Elizabeth "in a new Interest of State, to side with the Protestants against those Potent Monarchs of the other Religion." Much against her will, she had to support Protestant rebels in France and the Netherlands against their legitimate sovereigns; the men of 1640 learnt much from Huguenot and Dutch political theory. In the sixteen-thirties Archbishop Laud explained Lord Saye and Sele's Puritanism solely by the fact that "the most part of my Lord Sayes estate . . . consisted in Church means." Laud was wrong about Saye and Sele's property, as it happened; but he was right about the tendency. Fear that Charles I was going to attempt in England the policy of resuming[6] church lands which he had initiated in Scotland and Ireland caused many gentlemen to support Parliament.

In 1641 it was undoubtedly fear of Catholicism that deprived the King, at various critical moments, of his natural allies, the peers: and it is reasonable to suppose that the hostility of these great landowners to Popery was not exclusively theological. In the Civil War the King would gladly have called in Irish, French, or Spanish help, but his advisers feared lest acceptance of large-scale Catholic aid should bring with it an English Edict of Restitution, for even some Catholics held monastic estates. Great landowners like the Marquis of Newcastle or the Earl of Derby, for all their social conservatism, were held to an uncompromising Protestantism by their former church property.

Thus across all the divisions of the English Civil War there remained this firm bond of economic interest linking the gentry on the two sides. It was strong enough to make Protestant Royalist landlords in Ireland accept the victory of the English Parliament rather than fight side by side with Irish Papists; it was strong enough to promote the Royalist landslide of 1659–60 the moment the Peace of the Pyrenees had set Catholic France and Spain free to inter-

vene, jointly or separately, on behalf of the exiled Stuarts. Charles II told the Pope in 1670 that many landowners were restrained from declaring themselves in favour of Catholicism solely by fears for their property. The same anxiety was used as an argument against a Roman Catholic successor by the proponents of the Exclusion Bill. A century and a half after the dissolution, James II, in introducing his Declaration of Indulgence, felt obliged to say explicitly that he had no intention of following the grant of toleration to Catholics by an attempt to recover monastic lands. It was still a real political issue, and had been for the intervening 150 years.

We can capture something of the anxieties of the time from Andrew Marvell's *Account of the Growth of Popery and Arbitrary Government in England*, published in 1677. Marvell is explaining how the Protestant religion is interwoven with the secular interest of "the people," a word which he uses in the Harringtonian sense to signify what we should more accurately call "the middle class."

"The Lands that were formerly given to superstitious Uses, having first been applied to the publick Revenue, and afterwards by several Alienations and Contracts distributed into private possession, the alteration of Religion would necessarily introduce a change of Property. *Nullum tempus occurrit ecclesiae,*[7] it would make a general Earth-quake over the Nation, and even now the Romish Clergy on the other side of the Water snuff up the savoury Odour of so many rich Abbies and Monasteries that belonged to their Predecessors. Hereby no considerable Estate in England but must have a piece torn out of it upon the Title of Piety, and the rest subject to be wholly forfeited upon the Account of Heresie. Another Chimney-Money of the old Peter-Pence must again be paid, as Tribute to the Pope, beside that which is established on His Majesty: and the People, instead of those moderate Tythes that are with too

---

[6] Taking them back into the possession and management of the Crown.

[7] "Time runs not against the Church."

much difficulty paid to their Protestant Pastors, will be exposed to all the exactions of the Court of Rome, and a thousand Artifices by which in former times they were used to drain away the Wealth of ours more than any other Nation. So that in conclusion, there is no Englishman that hath a Soul, a Body, or an Estate to save, that Loves either God, his King or his Country, but is by all those Tenures bound, to the best of his Power and Knowledge, to maintain the Established Protestant Religion."

Party divisions were forgotten in 1688 as rapidly as they had been in 1660: for again liberty and property seemed to be at stake. After 1688 "the Protestant interest" and "England" came to be used as interchangeable terms.

In the sphere of ideas too the economic changes resulting from the Reformation acted as a dissolvent. Men learnt that church property was not sacrosanct, that traditional ecclesiastical institutions could disappear without the world coming to an end; that laymen could remodel not only the economic and political structures of the Church but also its doctrine — if they possessed political power. Protestant theology undermined the unique sacred character of the priest, and elevated the self-respect of his congregation. This helped men to question a divine right to tithes, the more so when tithes were paid to lay impropriators. Preaching became more important than the sacraments; and so men came to wonder what right non-preaching ministers, or absentees, had to be paid by their congregations. It took a long time to follow out these new lines of thought to their logical conclusions; but ultimately they led men very far indeed. By spreading ideas of sectarian voluntarism they prepared the way for the Revolution of 1640, and trained its more radical leaders.

In that Revolution episcopacy was abolished, bishops' and cathedral lands confiscated, the payment of tithes challenged. The radicals rejected not only Henry VIII's episcopal hierarchy but the whole idea of a state church. "O the great judgments of God!" Windebanke had exclaimed when contemplating the paradoxical outcome of the Henrician Reformation. Henry VIII had denied the supremacy of the Pope; he had confiscated church property; and he had allowed the Scriptures to be translated into English. These challenges to the authoritarianism, to the wealth and to the propaganda monopoly of the Church opened doors wider than was perhaps intended. A century later the authority first of King, then of Parliament, was challenged in the name of the people; the social justification of all private property was called in question; and speculation about the nature of the state and the rights of the people went to lengths which ultimately terrified the victorious Parliamentarians into recalling King, House of Lords, and bishops to help them to maintain law and order. By that date Windebanke had died in the exile to which the Revolution had condemned him, but not before he had openly proclaimed himself a Catholic. So he paid tribute to the superior wisdom of the Church which, Protestants said, believed that "ignorance is the mother of devotion."

SUGGESTIONS FOR ADDITIONAL READING

The literature on the Henrician Reformation is too vast to be dealt with here comprehensively. For that reason this bibliography is intended to guide the student in the direction of the most recent authoritative books and articles about the reign of Henry VIII, the chief problems pertaining to reform and Reformation in the several senses revealed in this anthology, and those figures besides the king who were important actors in the drama. The pursuit of any more detailed inquiries must rest on the *Bibliography of British History, Tudor Period, 1485–1603*, second edition (Oxford, 1959), edited by Conyers Read, and such shorter but useful guides as Lacey B. Smith, "The Taste for Tudors," *Studies in the Renaissance*, VII (1960), 167–83.

On Wolsey and the failure of reform in the years of his greatness the most valuable single book is still A. F. Pollard, *Wolsey* (London, 1929), though J. S. Brewer's *The Reign of Henry VIII*, 2 vols. (London, 1884) is basic to any understanding of politics and diplomacy to 1530. Special studies on the problems confronting Henry VIII and his ministers are legion. Among them, however, Margaret Aston, "Lollardy and Reformation: Survival or Revival," *History*, XLIX (1964), 149–70, is most stimulating on matters of heterodoxy among ordinary Englishmen, as is J. A. F. Thompson, *The Later Lollards* (Oxford, 1965). F. R. H. Du Boulay's "The Fifteenth Century," in *The English Church and the Papacy in the Middle Ages,* ed. C. H. Lawrence (London, 1965), provides an excellent survey of this critical relationship. On the growth of anticlerical sentiment and Hunne's case, Arthur Ogle, *The Tragedy of the Lollard's Tower* (Oxford, 1949) is often stimulating, though recent articles have somewhat altered our knowledge of this matter.

On the divorce as the immediate occasion of the Reformation, the best general treatment is Garrett Mattingly's beautifully written *Catherine of Aragon* (Boston, 1941). The crisis in Wolsey's career which the "King's great matter" represented has provoked sharp partisan discussion, the leading example being James Gairdner's "The fall of Cardinal Wolsey," in *Transactions of the Royal Historical Society,* 2nd series, XIII (1899), 75–102. A work dealing with some consequences of the way in which the royal problem provided critics of the Church with a parliamentary platform is G. R. Elton, "The Commons Supplication Against the Ordinaries," *English Historical Review* LXVI (1951), 507–34.

From the divorce flowed both the schism with Rome and the royal supremacy as well as the complicated rewriting of the treason laws, of which Thomas More was the chief victim. Among the most useful works here are: W. H. Dunham, Jr., "Regal Power and the Rule of Law: A Tudor Paradox," *Journal of British Studies*, III (1964), 24–56; L. B. Smith, "English Treason Trials and Confessions in the Sixteenth Century," *Journal of the History of Ideas,* XV (1954), 471–98; as well as the book of F. L. Van Baumer, *The Early Tudor Theory of Kingship* (Yale, 1940). But the most provocative contributions have certainly come from G. R. Elton, whose *Tudor Revolution in Government* (Cambridge, 1953) and numerous articles have triggered a controversy about the role of Thomas Cromwell and also the notion of sovereignty in the 1530's. These arguments can be followed in the pages of *Past and Present* from 1963 to 1965.

Traditionally, the Pilgrimage of Grace and the dissolution of the monasteries have been discussed as effect and cause. Recent works on these features of the Reformation in England have done much to cast doubt on earlier assumptions. By far the most stimulating works other than Knowles' books are the following: Alexander Savine, *English Monasteries on the Eve of the Dissolution* (Oxford, 1909); G. Baskerville, *English Monks and the Suppression of the Monasteries* (London, 1937), and Joan Simon, *Education and Society in Tudor England* (Cambridge, 1966). The entire controversy about monastic spoils and the gentry lies outside of the scope of this book and is gladly left to simmer. But the Northern Rising of 1536–37 cannot be put aside. Ruth and M. H. Dodds, *The Pilgrimage of Grace,* 2 vols. (Cambridge, 1915), provides the best narrative of events. A gifted historian, H. M. F. Prescott, has explored the interior history of that upheaval in her chronicle-novel, *The Man on a Donkey* (London, 1952), and every student of the Reformation should sample this wonderful book. On quite another level are the numerous works by A. G. Dickens illuminating Northern society, among them the masterful *Lollards and Protestants in the Diocese of York,* excerpted above, and his "Aspects of Intellectual Transition Among Parish Clergy," *Archiv für Reformationsgeschichte,* XLIII (1952), 51–69.

Reformation scholarship, while still often exhibiting partisans as unable to comprehend their opponents' views has advanced significantly in recent years in the areas of dogma and doctrine. Certainly E. G. Rupp's *The English Protestant Tradition* (Cambridge, 1947) is judicious, while O. Clebsch, *England's Earliest Protestants* (Yale, 1965), though less so, casts much light on the purely English Protestantism of early reformers. Apart from studies of particular "moderates," "conservatives" and men of the "advanced" party, L. B. Smith has written a fine book on *Tudor Prelates and Politics* (Princeton, 1953), in which the entire episcopal bench is subjected to analysis. A. G. Dickens, *The English Reformation* (London, 1964), contains lucid chapters on doctrinal matters. But these issues must perhaps be best studied in the lives of individual reformers and politicians of the period. Pride of place must go to the greatest men: R. W. Chambers, *Thomas More* (London, 1935); A. G. Dickens, *Thomas Cromwell and the English Reformation* (London, 1959); J. A. Muller, *Stephen Gardiner* (New York, 1926), and Jasper Ridley, *Thomas Cromwell* (Oxford, 1962). Among the so-called "reform" party, H. L. Chester's *Hugh Latimer* (Philadelphia, 1952) may be commended along with A. J. Slavin's study of *Politics and Profit* (Cambridge, 1966). Charles Sturge's *Cuthbert Tunstal* (London, 1938) is a good book about that learned and complex bishop. But by far the most intriguing work about the "moderates," and one which casts doubt on the use of all party labels in the 1530's, is the recent book of J. K. McConica, *English Humanists and Reformation Politics* (Oxford, 1965), in which it is argued that the entire reform community in England was Erasmian in its goals and methods and that its political leader was Thomas Cromwell. While not denying that the unity of the group was shattered between 1532 and 1535, McConica argues powerfully that we must separate the accidents of politics from the complex questions of reform and avoid attaching party labels prematurely. To some extent these same views are championed by Arthur Ferguson, *The Articulate Citizen of the English Renaissance* (Durham, N.C., 1965), examining the social thought of the era, as well as older books by W. G. Zeeveld, *Foundations of Tudor Policy* (London, 1948) and Fritz Caspari, *Humanism and the Social Order in Tudor England* (Chicago, 1954).

In what directions the frontiers of Reformation research may yet move is a question the answer to which depends on what has already been accomplished. Suffice it to say that the character of the main actors will continue to fascinate, as can be seen in G. R. Elton's essay *Henry VIII* (London, 1963), and the forthcoming *Henry VIII* of J. J. Scarisbrick. It also seems certain that the social and economic implications of reform will be pursued vigorously. Perhaps it is the internal politics of reform and the enforcement of the Reformation that most need study at the center. Increasingly, however, historians are declaring themselves dissatisfied with Reformation history written in terms of high policy, constitutionalism, and diplomacy; as the search for understanding goes on, students may turn with rapt interest to the people below the first rank and to social groups and communities less august than Parliament and Convocation. The future may lie with local historians who write Reformation history on the level of the shire or even the parish.